THE GREAT AND INIMITABLE
JUNE BYERS

By John Cosper

Copyright 2023 by Eat Sleep Wrestle, LLC

All Rights Reserved

www.eatsleepwrestle.com

Front cover designed by James Duncan.

Image on back cover courtesy Wil Byers.

For Sydney and Desiree

On the set with Kamille (as June Byers) and June's granddaughter Kay Parker. Courtesy Kay Parker.

FOREWORD

The month of May was coming to an end. In fact, it was the very last evening of May leading into June. A very strange coincidence that is not lost on me in retrospect. But, seeing as I don't really believe in coincidence, maybe fate had a hand in bringing me and June, no, not the month, together. I had just received a message that I landed my first ever movie role. I would be playing none other than June Byers.

Now, admittedly, the only reason I had heard of June's name before all of this was because I was a current NWA Women's Champion. A title that June had once proudly held. At the time I received the role, she was the one woman in front of me as I was working to etch my name into the top five all time longest reigns list for that title. I was number six, June number five.

In the film that has not come out yet at the time of me writing this, June is undoubtedly the villain in the story. The movie is about the life and career of Mildred Burke. A woman that you will come to find out in this book was one of June's fiercest rivalries. And what's a great hero without a great villain?

When I read about what they wanted for this role, June was described as a tall, muscular, rough and tough Texas girl. Well, being from the south, and being a bit of a roughhouser myself, I knew I would be the perfect fit. But I wanted to know all I could know about June Byers to really do her justice. Through many hours of research, some being provided by Mr. Cosper, I found out all about June Byers. Although I did my best at portraying the ice-cold bad guy for the film, I knew that wasn't exactly the case for the real-life June. She had humble beginnings and a kind heart that those closest to her knew. She was a beast in the ring, and an absolute show-stopping beauty outside of it. Even in the old black and white pictures, her smile radiated through showing what a true lady she was. June was a classy woman in every sense of the word.

I hope this book that John has written shows everyone the sides of June that fans on the inside of the wrestling arena never got to see. We all play characters in this wacky world of wrestling, and the best ones are those that blur the lines of what is fact and what is fiction, what is reality and what is all just a facade. June perfectly portrayed that. I truly think June will be up in heaven smiling that she left such an imprint on the business. That her wrestling persona has stood the test of time. So much so that her character is vital to the plot of the film about Burke. The final scene the movie works towards is based around wanting to see Mildred defeat June. David and Goliath in a sense. That's the presence June had. She knew that it took a great heel to make people care about a babyface and elicit emotion when that underdog could come out on top. She knew how to get others over and in doing so got herself over.

I spoke some with her granddaughter, Kay, and she could not have said more wonderful things about her late grandmother. She loved her dearly and she had a huge influence on her life. There are many other instances in this book where you will see what a vibrant, strong and truly extraordinary person June Byers was.

I would personally like to thank June for everything she contributed to the business and the way she paved the path for women like me. Oftentimes this era of women's wrestling is overlooked. People talk about a "Woman's Revolution" happening in recent years of wrestling, but they forget that in the days of Byers, Burke, Mae, Elvira and more, those women were drawing better than the boys. It was a statistical fact. Main eventing more often than not. June Byers was a major player in all of that and someone that I am elated is receiving more recognition in the modern era. I know her family and friends must be so proud!

Kailey Latimer
("The Brickhouse" Kamille)
September 27, 2023

WHAT'S HER LINE?

On a warm summer night in August of 1953, a tall, elegant woman walked onto the stage of a television studio and wrote June B. Wolfe in perfect cursive on a chalkboard. Many viewers at home had no clue who this woman was or, as the panel on the show would soon ask, what her "line" might be. But some did. True, the last name Wolfe might have created some doubts, but that smile and "June B." were all they needed to answer the question.

From Baltimore to Houston to Seattle, men and women nearly fell out of their easy chairs, pointing at the black and white screen in the large, wooden cabinet that formed the center of the family room.

"That's her! Remember her?"

They weren't fooled by her appearance, wearing a dress and cloak along with a pendant necklace and holding white gloves as she shook hands with panelists Steve Allen, Arlene Francis, Bennett Cerf, and Dorothy Kilgallen of the popular CBS show *What's My Line?* They knew those hands had been around the necks of many, many women. They'd seen those very hands strike, lift, toss the likes of Elvira Snodgrass, Mae Young, Mars Bennett, Violet Viann, and Nell Stewart across the ring.

She had a million dollar smile and an elegant manner. Her hair was perfectly quaffed, and her jewelry sparkled even through the black and white telecast. She looked every bit the part of a refined lady.

The loyal, hearty fans of the smoke-filled arenas were not fooled. They guffawed as the panelists tried to guess her profession, mentioning everything from a rodeo queen to someone who dances with dogs. They were in the ballpark, but not close enough. Watching on the monitors, the studio audience was let in on the secret at the same time as the viewers at home when two words appeared over her face:

PROFESSIONAL WRESTLER.

"I told you!" said a man in Cincinnati, slamming his fist on the armrest. "I told you it was her!"

"Her who?" said the wife from the other room.

"It's June Byers!" he shouted. "Don't you remember? She kicked the living hell out of Lilly Bitter at the Arena a few months ago!"

Some viewers were not so pleased seeing the woman they hated on screen, smiling and being treated like a celebrity. The Hat Pin Marys of the world, those sweet, little old grannies who turned into profanity-spewing witches at ringside, stared daggers at the long, tall Texan, wishing they could reach through the screen, grab hold of those tight curls, and yank her hair out by the roots.

The studio audience might have been surprised and delighted to learn she was a professional wrestler, but not Hat Pin Mary. Hat Pin Mary wanted her dead, broken, busted, and bloodied.

June savored the crowd reaction as they screamed, cheered, laughed, and applauded. She laughed heartily as John Charles Daly remarked how the panelists, bright as they were, had their work cut out for them.

Steve Allen kicked off the questioning. The future host of *The Tonight Show* asked June if she was involved in some sort of service work. June said yes. He asked if she could perform the service on him. June laughed, as did the crowd, and said yes.

"Does what you do bring you in direct contact with the people for whom you do it?" he asked.

"Yes," said June.

"Could you affect them in any way personally, like their well-being or their appearance?" asked Mr. Allen.

June and Mr. Daly exchanged a look as the crowd laughed again. June nodded and replied, "Yes."

"Are the people for whom you perform these services ever in a position other than standing?"

Again, June replied, "Yes."

"Might what you do ever cause a slight degree of discomfort or pain?"

"Yes," said June.

"Yes, there are some who might feel discomfort as a result," added Mr. Daly.

Mr. Allen asked, "You work directly with the body?"

"You might say that Mrs. Wolfe works directly with the body, yes," said Mr. Daly.

"Do you ever work with the mouth?" asked Mr. Allen.

The audience giggled as June answered, "Yes."

"Would I ever go to you if I wanted to have some teeth removed?"

The audience roared. June looked at Mr. Daly. She wanted to say yes, but Mr. Daly interjected. "I can't see you going to Mrs. Wolfe to have your teeth removed," he said, giving Mr. Allen the first no of the game and sending the questioning over to actress Arlene Francis.

Ms. Francis was much more attuned with June B. Wolfe's true line of work. She asked June to confirm that she not only comes in contact with another person but that the other person does not benefit from what she does. Mr. Daly gave June a nod, and she replied, "Yes."

"Do you handle more than one person at a time?" asked Ms. Francis.

"Yes," said June.

"On some occasions," added Mr. Daly.

"Do they learn anything from you?" asked Mrs. Francis.

June didn't let Mr. Daly step in this time. With a raised brow she quickly replied, "Yes they do," sending Mr. Daly into a laughing fit.

Ms. Francis lost her chance to continue asking questions on a technicality, turning the questioning over to Bennett Cerf. The wily publisher had June's occupation within just a few questions, guessing she was, indeed, a lady wrestler.

Mr. Daly informed the panel, and specifically Steve Allen, that Mrs. Wolfe's full name was June Byers and that she was in fact the World Champion. Byers had been recognized as such by many promoters following her April 14, 1953 win in a championship tournament held in Baltimore, Maryland. She had yet to defeat the reigning world champion Mildred Burke, but change was in the air, both in the ring and in the locker room. Burke's days as the queen of the ring were coming to an end, and June Byers, who at the time was married to the son of women's wrestling promoter Billy Wolfe, had staked her claim to the throne.

Casual wrestling fans can be forgiven if they've never heard the name June Byers. Even if they know of Mildred Burke, who was arguably the greatest women's star of all time, they may not know the story of June Byers.

In the 1980s, one regional wrestling promotion rose to national prominence. They did so by securing national broadcasting contracts while raiding the other territories of their top stars. By the middle part of the 1990s, they were one of only two surviving promotions, and by 2001, only one remained.

The third generation promoter at the head of this conglomerate was tight with a woman named Lillian Ellison, better known to fans as The Fabulous Moolah. A long-time claimant to the Women's World Championship and the predominant trainer/booker for lady wrestlers of her time, Moolah used her platform with the WWE to portray herself as the greatest women's champion in history.

Never mind that she never worked two-out-of-three falls marathons night after night. Never mind that she never sold out houses like Burke and Byers. Never mind that she, unlike her predecessors, was never a main event draw. Just as her boss rewrote the history of the business at large in his family's image, Moolah rewrote the women's portion in hers.

Moolah's most egregious lie appears on pages 106 and 107 of

the hardcover edition of her self-titled autobiography. After laying claim to being the women's world champion thanks to a tournament held by Vince McMahon, Sr., Moolah tells the story of how she faced and defeated an unretired June Byers in Louisville, Kentucky to become the true, undisputed Women's World Champion.

"The bell rang, and she instantly knew she had her hands full," wrote Moolah. "Around the time I smashed her face into the turnbuckle, I knew I had her."

She never had her.

Moolah never faced June Byers for the Women's World Championship in Louisville.

She never faced June Byers for the Women's World Championship anywhere.

Moolah was spinning the tale of her victory over June as early as 1955. In a *Wrestling Revue* interview with Jim Melby that took place in 1984, June set the record straight. "I did wrestle Moolah early in her career before she adopted that title, and beat her. She never did beat me in the ring. When I retired I was still the champion."

Granted, June's claim to the title has often been disputed, especially by Burke's biggest fans. The match between Burke and Byers in 1954 did not go to two falls as agreed. Burke lost one fall, which she blamed on a bad knee, but the match was stopped before a second fall could take place.

Still, only one woman can lay claim to being the successor to Mildred Burke, and that's June Byers. For ten years after that hot night in Atlanta, June defended her title with honor, retiring as an unconquered, never beaten champion.

June Byers was many things to many people. She was an icon, a representation of women stepping out of the traditional roles to become whatever and whomever they wanted in life. She was a pariah, a natural heel that, despite her championship gold, they would never cheer and always hate. And that, I am sure, was perfectly okay with her.

To Billy Wolfe she was his last gasp, his last chance to continue his dominance of women's wrestling.

June Byers was all these things and more. She was a trailblazer and a pioneer. She was a shrewd and savvy businesswoman who had a long, successful career outside wrestling. She was a strong, daring mother who took a risk to make a better life for her son. She was an active and proud grandmother who continues to inspire generations that follow her footsteps.

To all these we add one more: she was unconquered. Undefeated. A woman who retired as the Women's World Wrestling Champion.

TEXAS BORN AND BRED

"Seven years ago when I was making 35 dollars a week in Houston I used to see the lady wrestlers when they came to town and nearly died when I saw the diamonds they were wearing."

The woman born DeAlva Eyvonnie Sibley dripped with diamonds herself as she told the story to United Press writer Scott Baillie. The two sat at a coffee counter in New York City, accompanied by women's wrestling impresario Billy Wolfe himself. Baillie admired the "ice" dripping from her fingers but also noted the cigarette clenched between two of those digits was the twelve cent variety.

Crossing her toned, shapely legs as she perched on her stool, June Byers went on. "I said to myself, 'If they can get all that just by wrestling, I'm all for it. Besides, I'm kind of athletic myself."

The future champion came into the world on May 25, 1922 in Houston, Texas. Her father was Arthur Sibley, a farmer who also worked as a house painter, and her mother was Ruby Lee Cook Sibley. At the time of her birth, the family already had seven boys and five girls — thirteen children in all. It's pretty typical that the youngest would work the hardest to stand out, to be seen. To be noticed.

It's also understandable that after twelve children, the couple had a difficult time settling on a name for the baby girl. It took a few weeks to settle on DeAlva Eyvonnie, a name many folks found difficult to pronounce. Some had already taken to calling the girl "June" since the month of May was now past and the girl remained unnamed. Though not her legal name, the nickname would stay with her for life.

At the age of eight, June's aunt and uncle took her to the City Auditorium in Houston. Completed in 1910, the 7,000 seat building on the corner of Texas Avenue and Louisiana Street was touted as the most modern auditorium in the state. City Auditorium hosted many legendary music performers and theatrical events over the years, but in the mid-1920s it became home to the weekly professional wrestling show held every Friday night.

Inspired by the wrestling shows that came to town sporadically from 1915 through 1923, a man named Julius Siegel began running shows weekly in the Auditorium. Under Julius and later his brother Morris Siegel, pro wrestling became one of the most popular events held at City Auditorium. Eight-year-old June likely saw stars like Rudy Dusek, Paul Jones, Dick Shikat, Jim Londos, Strangler Lewis, and a man who would later make a huge impact in Houston, Paul Boesch.

By the time June turned eight, Julius had left the promotion in the hands of his brother Morris. Morris did not have the knowledge of the business like his brother did, but he'd keep the wrestling promotion going throughout the Great Depression and World War II. He'd also be instrumental in aiding June's entry into the business.

June's aunt and uncle had a pair of close friends they always met at the matches: Bell Roberts and her husband Ottoway, better known to his friends as Shorty. The five would take in the show and then go up the street to the Chinese Consulate Restaurant, where Morris Siegel and many of his crew also ate after the show.

Through these many dinners, Morris Siegel struck up a friendship with "Shorty" Roberts. Siegel had a ranch in New Waverly, Texas, and he asked Roberts to take charge of the ranch for him. Roberts agreed, solidifying his place in Siegel's inner circle.

June Byers would often credit her "Uncle" Ottoway Roberts as the man who first trained her to become a pro wrestler, saying it was he who put her on a body-building program at the tender age of seven. While Ottoway was not her blood uncle, she certainly came to see the man as an uncle thanks to his close friendship with her aunt and uncle. It's very likely Ottoway did some wrestling himself and may have been one of many Houston grapplers to help June learn the ropes, so to speak.

June spoke to Jim Melby in 1984 about her early grappling experience. "By the time I was thirteen years old I could beat every other kid in the neighborhood in a row. I wasn't a bully or a toughie, though. When I went to high school I could beat all of the boys on the wrestling team. I went to a country school, and those fellows were pretty tough."

June gives Ottoway Roberts the nod in most interviews as her initial trainer, but in 1951, she told Helen Sylvia of *Wrestling and TV Sports* she also trained with Carl Davids and Bobby Managoff. It's likely she stepped in the ring with many more men over the years, learning from whomever was willing to teach her.

June's "official" biography varies from interview to interview, and many of the details cannot be fully verified. In a 1961 interview with *The Ring*, June said that she wrestled as an amateur in high school and college. She won the girls wrestling championship at Klein High School, and while her sex did not allow her to join the college team, the coach allowed her to work out with the boys.

June also spoke about other sports outside of wrestling, but it's often hard to tell what's fact and fiction from the interviews and promotional stories that came out later in her life. One promoter said she'd played girls football. Speaking with a Kansas City reporter in 1946, June said she tried softball and became a pitcher. "ut the manager thought I was trying to run the team, so I quit."

The Texas girl loved horses and horseback riding and enjoyed the sport even into adulthood. She told the same Kansas City reporter she had a horse named Chestnut back home.

Granddaughter Debra Nowaski recalls a funny story about June and her horse. "She was dating a young man in the neighborhood and one of her friends told her that her boyfriend was in the neighborhood icehouse with another girl. June grabbed her bridle and quirt and hopped on the horse and took off. She opened the front door of the bar, rode in on horseback, whacked the guy with her quirt, and rode back out. She would tell this story and throw her head back and just laugh. Needless to say, that was the end of their friendship."

June was only sixteen when she became a wife and mother. Her husband, Allie Parr, was ten years older than June. The couple named their daughter Jewel. Parr knew about June's love for the wrestling ring. In fact, she was already training with the boys at the arena. But Allie was looking for a housewife and mother. If he hoped to tame the girl by giving her a home and a child, he realized quickly that he was with the wrong person. The couple divorced.

By June's account, she attended college at Rice University, a private research university located in Houston. Although in Division I in athletics, the school has long been trapped in the shadow of Texas, Texas A&M, and the other high profile sports programs in the state. Their greatest claim to fame is the Marching Owl Band, or the MOB, known for their snazzy, throwback mobster attire as well as their smoking rendition of "Louie Louie." If youu've seen the movie *The Naked Gun* and remember the scene where a man is trampled by the USC Trojans marching band, that's Rice's band playing the music, not USC's.

June's degree was in geology, and she went to work with the Texas Company in their geophysical laboratory. She enjoyed her work, but the money was low, especially when compared to the numbers she heard about the lady wrestlers.

June gave domestic life a second shot when she married Henry Thomas Byers. The couple had a son they named William Henry Byers, born January 1, 1942 in Harris, Texas. Yet even with two small children in the house, June couldn't shake her desire to become a pro wrestler.

In a 1963 interview with *The Ring* magazine, June spoke about having to go back to work after her husband passed away in a house fire. Henry Byers did indeed die in a fire caused by a gas leak in his apartment, but by the time of his death, June was already a claimant to the world championship. Henry Byers passed away in 1953, eight years after his wife began her wrestling career in earnest. June's story of becoming desperate was false, but even in 1963, divorcing one husband, let alone two, to become a professional wrestler would have been hard for the general public to accept.

June Byers was never meant to be a stay-at-home wife. She wanted everything that becoming a professional wrestler could give her: money, fine jewelry, fancy clothes, flashy cars. And nothing, not marriage, not motherhood, was going to stand in her way.

She had allies. Ottoway Roberts believed in her. So did Morris Siegel. So did Paul Boesch. A native New Yorker, Boesch had been in and out of the ring for many years and made many appearances in Houston, where he likely met June at one of the post-match dinners. When injuries forced Boesch to hang up his boots, Morris Siegel reached out, asking him to come on as a consultant and the announcer for the weekly radio broadcast. Boesch became a fixture of the Houston wrestling scene for decades to come. Boesch, Siegel, and Roberts were keen to see June succeed in the business.

Exactly how Billy Wolfe and June met is another one of those gray areas. In that same 1961 interview with *The Ring*, June claimed she met Billy while attending the matches at City Auditorium with a girl friend. Wolfe had come looking for her, having heard tales of her exploits in the ring, and he wanted to give her a tryout.

The August 1954 edition of *Boxing and Wrestling* describes a scene at City Auditorium that may very well have attracted Billy Wolfe's attention. June was sitting ringside, as she always did, laying into a 300 pound heel named Killer Karl Davis one night. Davis took exception to June's taunting and invited her into the ring, telling her in essence to put up or shut up.

To the crowd's delight, June bounded into the ring and slapped a Hammerlock on Davis. She converted the hold into a Full Nelson, causing Davis to cry out for help from "the police, the Decency League, and the Society for the Prevention of Cruelty to Wrestlers."

In his biography of Mildred Burke, *Queen of the Ring*, Jeff Leen puts Billy Wolfe at ringside the night June had her altercation with Davis. Although dwarfed by the size of Davis, June was taller than most of the girls already in his employ. He recognized the skills. He saw her beauty. He saw box office.

The Killer Karl Davis story fits with the narrative most of the ladies from her era put forth in their official biographies. Every single one of them came in on day one and whipped someone bigger, stronger, and more experienced. Mae Young claimed to have pinned both Gladys "Kill 'Em" Gillem and Elvira Snodgrass in a matter of seconds before she ever had a lesson. Mildred Burke, likewise, claimed to have whipped an eighteen-year-old boy, one of Billy's star students at the time, without being taught one hold.

As fanciful as these tales are, you have to question their credibility when compared with the tales of more modern stars. Hulk Hogan had his leg broken on day one, just to test him. Dr. D David Schultz worked like a dog from sunrise to sunset on Herb Welch's farm before being taken to the barn and twisted in knots by his teacher every night. And just ask any man who ever set foot in Stu Hart's Dungeon how their first time on the mat went. The screams of a thousand wannabe wrestlers are trapped in the walls of the house that overlooks Calgary.

Sure, it's possible Mildred Burke, at 115 pounds, whipped a trained eighteen-year-old. Yes, it's possible Mae Young pinned two veteran shooters in seconds. But it's much more likely the queens of the kayfabe era took their fair share of lumps before showing any sign of success.

June would be no exception to the rule, but by the time her public sparring match with Davis took place, she'd logged countless hours in the ring with other men. She started locking up in her early teens. She knew the holds. She'd probably pulled the Hammerlock into a Full Nelson on Karl Davis dozens of times in practice.

And June, by all accounts, already had a fair deal of skill in knowing how to shoot. By the time Billy Wolfe laid eyes on her, she'd have had the skills to fair a hell of a lot better than Mildred Burke and Mae Young against another shooter.

One can't overlook Morris Siegel and Paul Boesch in this part of the story. The two men certainly had a hand in recommending June to Billy Wolfe. The incident with Karl Davis might have even been staged for his benefit.

June had to make a very difficult sacrifice to make her dream happen. While Mildred Burke had been able to pursue her dream with a child in tow, June had two, and anyone who has raised children will tell you that two small children are more than double the work of just one.

Uncertain she could pursue her dream with two babies in tow, June turned to Ottoway and Belle Roberts. The couple had been unable to have children of their own, and June asked if they might adopt her daughter Jewel. The couple gladly agreed.

June's mother would care for her son from time to time in those early days of training, but William, or as she called him "Billy Boy," would grow up on the road with his mother. She would also keep the last name she shared with Billy Boy, combining it with her childhood nickname to become her in-ring moniker.

June Byers was ready to take on all comers.

THE NEW GIRL

Business was booming for Billy Wolfe. The former wrestler turned women's wrestling advocate struck gold in the mid-1930s when a small town Kansas waitress named Millie Bliss demanded he teach her to wrestle. Wolfe wanted nothing to do with the girl. Only 5'2", barely 115 pounds, and a single mother, she refused to take no for an answer.

Millie endured every challenge he threw at her. He took her out on the carnival circuit, where she took on all comers. He got her a match with Clara Mortenson, the Women's World Champion. She won the title, and other than a few short weeks in 1938 (when Betty Nichols, aka Gutherine Fuller, aka Elvira Snodgrass) snatched the title from her in Ohio, she would reign supreme for the next sixteen years.

Wolfe and Burke got married. If there was ever any love or romance between them, it ended soon after the wedding. For most of their marriage, they would sleep in separate bedrooms. Burke spent many of those years sleeping with Wolfe's son, George William "G. Bill" Wolfe. Billy Wolfe, Sr., would sleep with whatever ladies in his employ would allow him, often in exchange for better spots on the wrestling cards.

Not long after Mildred Burke became champion, the world went to war. Many of the top male wrestlers left the ring to serve their country. With the majority of the top male stars gone, Mildred Burke became a main event attraction, rising to a level of prominence she would hold long after the war had ended. She wrestled two out of three falls every night against Billy Wolfe's top talent: Mae Weston, Mae Young, Gladys "Kill 'Em" Gillem, and Elvira Snodgrass.

She made big money. He made more money. The ladies wrestling Burke made good money too, and a good chunk of their winnings went right through their pockets and into Billy's.

The success of women's wrestling in the early 1940s created more demand. It also inspired more women to pursue wrestling. Eager young women, many with stories that echoed Burke's, approached Billy and the ladies at shows, asking how they could give wrestling a shot. It was a buyer's market for Billy Wolfe.

June Byers was a no brainer. She was tall, fit, and athletic. She was a leftie, a trait often mentioned by sports writers who loved to extol the unique advantage of being a southpaw. She had a winning smile and statuesque figure.

Billy Wolfe's base of operations was in Columbus, Ohio. The boss assigned Mae Young to teach June how to play the villain, seeing her as a perfect foil for Mildred Burke. Wolfe also gave June one of his signature moves, a "cupped chest lick," a hard chop to the chest that sounded painful. It often was when June delivered it.

June Byers listed her public wrestling debut as taking place in Wilmington, Delaware in 1944. Odds are she was taking bumps in front of a crowd in 1944, honing her skills away from the eyes of the wrestling beat writers, but it wasn't until January 9, 1945, that she made her professional debut in Wilmington.

June's opponent that night was Mae Weston, a savvy veteran who started wrestling Mildred Burke in 1938. Her career lasted until the mid-1970s, when she became Maw Bass, manager and matriarch to the notorious Ron and Don Bass.

Promoter Jimmy Houghton added the girls match to a card headlined by "world champion" Babe Sharkey, who was putting his title on the line against Don Evans. Sharkey was billed as a Texan but actually came from Pennsylvania. He was known later in his career as Hard Boiled Hannigan. June lost that first bout in eleven minutes and fifteen seconds.

The following night, June got her first taste of tag team action. Her partner was Rose Evans, real-life sister to Mae Weston, who had been known by many other names including Babe Gordon. The two tangled with Irene Jordan and Nell Stewart, a ravishing blonde with movie star looks who was already sharing a bed with Billy Wolfe. The girls were featured in the main event before a crowd of 5,200. June came out on the losing end for the second night in a row.

As a newcomer, June took a number of defeats that first month. She dropped matches to Mae Young in Florida, one in Tampa and one in Miami. From Miami, June had to trek all the way up the East Coast to Maine for a tag match against Celia Blevins and Mae Weston. Her partner for that evening was Elvira Snodgrass.

Arguably the number two woman in the business at that time, Elvira hailed from Varnado, Louisiana and entered the business in the late 1930s. Billy Wolfe often put new girls on the road with Elvira, not only to show them the ropes but make sure they were tough enough to make it.

Elvira and June were victorious in the January 29 tag match in Portland, and June suddenly found herself in the win column more often than not. She defeated Mae Weston in Memphis and St. Louis. She topped Elvira Snodgrass in Atlanta and Memphis.

The earliest promo photos of June contrast greatly with the image she later made famous. Her hair is down and shoulder length. She wears a sleeveless top that covers her belly along with a pair of boyish trunks. Most striking, her face is hard and stoic, devoid of any hint of a smile. The serious, scowling look worked well for Mildred Burke and a few other ladies, but June would not scowl for very long. Try as she might, it just wasn't who she was.

"Mae Young and I back when we first met June thought she must have come from a dentist's family, because she had such pretty teeth," said Theresa Theis, another member of Wolfe's troupe. "She was always smiling even when she was putting a painful hold on an opponent." That smile would become her signature, setting her apart as much as the "come hither" gaze of her contemporary Nell Stewart.

June's radiant smile may have inspired some of the early billing that hyped her as a Hollywood starlet turned wrestler. Miami promoter Charlie Laye told *The Miami News* that June Byers had just filmed a couple of shorts in Hollywood. *The Journal Herald* of Dayton said she was one of the top names of Earl Carroll's *Vanities*, a popular Broadway production enjoying a revival at the time thanks to a feature film of the same name. *Vanities* launched the careers of some show business legends including Sophie Tucker, Ted Healy, W.C. Fields, Milton Berle, and Harold Arlen, but June Byers was never one of the 108 girls seen onstage during the show's run.

"Always a lover of sports," the *Herald* went on, "she became interested in wrestling after seeing Mildred Burke in one of her ring appearances in California. Miss Byers took matters seriously and it was not until after several months of diligent training that she had her first match."

Another reason for the Hollywood angle might have been June's spot on the card. Even though she was a new name to the fans, she was often working the semi-main or main event alongside Elvira, Mae Young, and Mae Weston. The War was still on, and women's wrestling was popular enough to draw in the main event, even if one of the competitors was a rookie. A rookie from Hollywood meant the girl was a looker, and that translated into ticket sales.

Some nights, the ladies were the whole show. June and Elvira worked a number of cards with two other ladies — usually Mae Young, Irene Jordan, or Ann Laverne — in which the girls would pair off to fill the main and semi-main events. If a third match was offered, the men were in the opener. They might get their names in the paper the day after, but at least one ad from Hastings, Massachusetts merely promised "One Other Good Match" on top of the women's double bill.

The ladies were money.

Irene Jordan worked a few of these double bills in the Midwest and New England. She was new to the business, like June, but she didn't last. One night in Holyoke, Massachusetts, she suffered the wrath of Mae Young when she wrapped Mae's right leg around her ribs. Young grabbed Jordan by the hair and punched her face until her eyes were both black. She then threw Jordan on the mat and pounded her face into the canvas. Jordan was taken to the hospital in Boston, where she was diagnosed with a concussion. She was released six weeks later, and she never resumed her wrestling career.

Ann Laverne, on the other hand, was a native of Canton, Ohio with a few years seasoning on her. Her first recorded match took place in 1941, and her last would not come until 1969 in Toledo. Ann had just as much fire and skill as Elvira and Mae, according to women's wrestling historian Chris Bergstrom. "She was the first woman to wrestle with cauliflower ears. She was a shooter, and tough as nails." She was also one more piece of iron, sharpening the skills of June Byers during her rookie year.

Ann had a daughter, Marie, who would also become a professional wrestler. Marie's father was also a wrestler, none other than Billy Wolfe himself.

June more than held her own at every turn. A newspaper in Palm Beach gave her a nickname made famous decades later by the great Beth Phoenix: the Glamazon. She was growing in confidence with every match while taking her lumps from some of the toughest women who would ever grace the squared circle.

During the summer June had the first of many, many singles matches with Nell Stewart. Nell was, in many ways, the antithesis to Mildred Burke. While Burke had a physique that appealed to men who liked their girls with muscles, Nell Stewart had more classic sex appeal with her 36-28-38 figure. Yet Nell was trained to work a roughhouse, rock 'em sock 'em style that contrasted with her movie star looks. Nell quickly gained popularity with the fans and became a major attraction.

Nell Stewart and June Byers would be linked together on many nights over the years, and not just as ring rivals. The two would compete for the favor of the boss. They both worked hard in the ring, in the gym, and on the road to prove they could be the heir to the reigning champion when the time came to pass the torch. But one would be left lying stunned on the mat when the moment of decision finally came.

June made her first appearances wrestling in Baltimore during October of 1945, defeating Elvira Snodgrass and Nell Stewart on consecutive weeks. Baltimore would become a significant place in the rivalry between Byers and Stewart, but in the fall of 1945, a truly life-changing moment took place not for June, but a soldier who suffered debilitating injuries while serving in France.

Baltimore promoter George M. Cavanaugh hosted a group of patients from the Newton D. Baker Hospital on one of those evenings when the ladies were in town. The girls were so popular with the troops, Cavanaugh asked Billy Wolfe if he'd mind sending a few of them to do a show at the hospital for the troops. Wolfe was happy to oblige, sending. June, Nell Stewart, Violet Viann, and Madge Evans.

The ladies arrived dressed to the nines, as always, each wearing a corsage. Nell, Violet, and Madge all sported roses, but June had chosen an orchid, a decision that would lead to an incredible moment.

The ladies made their way from one ward to the next, greeting the soldiers while enduring the wolf calls, whistles, and flirting from the grateful troops. They visited with amputees and then paralytics, who were all in one ward together. It was there that nurses observed one of the young men staring intently at June. Everywhere the lady went, his eyes followed.

One of the nurses observed this and pulled June aside. She told June that the boy had been injured in France and had not spoken a word since being taken off the battlefield. The nurse asked June to go say hello and to try to get the boy to speak.

Tough as nails in the ring, June Byers walked over and stood beside the young man. She noticed his eyes were fixed on her corsage, and she told him gently it was an orchid.

The soldier said, "My mother used to grow them. I wonder if she does now."

June sat down on the edge of the bed, and the two began to talk. She spent the rest of the time she had before the show, giving the boy her full attention. When it was time to go, she removed the corsage and pinned it to the boy's night clothes. She bent over the bed and whispered something in his ear, then she tenderly brushed her lips against his.

As June made her way out of the ward, the nurses saw the boy wipe a tear from his eyes. The lady wrestler had done for him in minutes what all the medicine in the world could not do. She had brought him back, mentally, from the frontlines to the home front. She had given him the first glimpse of hope he'd seen in weeks.

Once the fans got to know June, the Hollywood backstory was dropped for good. She didn't need it. Holding her own against the toughest ladies in the business, June Byers made a name all her own. Over the summer, Oklahoma promoter Leroy McGuirk pushed June as a tough grappling gal from Louisville, Kentucky, but that too would fall by the wayside. June Byers was a Texas beauty through and through.

As she told the *Cincinnati Inquirer,* "I'm just a little cowgirl from the lone prairie." A cowgirl who could knock your teeth out!

June wrestled at the American Legion in Lake Worth, Florida on November 19, 1945. She finished Mae Gordon off with a series of flying tackles after eighteen minutes of intense action that more than rivaled the men on the card.

The cameras for Movietone News captured the action at ringside. Film producer William Fox, founder of Fox Films, created Fox Movietone News in 1919, creating silent, moving picture broadcasts that played in movie theaters. The company added sound to its newsreels in 1928. Fox Films merged with Twentieth Century Pictures in 1935 to become 20th Century Fox, but Movietone continued to produce newsreels for the screen until 1963.

Newsreels were a great way to introduce the sport to new eyes. In the days before television, they gave many men, women, and children their first look at professional wrestling. Many viewers were appalled by the site of women in skimpy costumes pulling hair and smacking each other around the ring, but others were intrigued enough to seek out their local wrestling promotion and check out the action in person.

The girl from Houston saw a lot of the Midwest and Southeast to finish out the year, working dates right up to the Christmas holiday in Ohio and picking up as soon as December 25 was past. Two days after Christmas in Shreveport, Louisiana, Rose Evans manhandled and pinned the "rookie" to win the first fall of their main event bout. Beaten but not beat, June Byers came back strong to win the second and third falls as well as the hearts of the Shreveport faithful. While she would specialize in playing the heel for most of her career, June knew how to turn on the charm and win over a crowd.

June returned a week later to face Mae Weston, Rose's real life sister, in a bout to determine who would get a title shot against champion Mildred Burke. The Louisiana fans were solidly in June's corner that night as women's wrestling filled the main event slot for the second week in a row. The victory, and the title shot, went to Mae Weston on that January evening, but June's day was coming.

BRIDESMAID

"I'm a rifle man in the New Galahad combat team known as the Mars Task Force." So began a letter to the editor of the *Evening World-Herald*, a newspaper based in Omaha, Nebraska. "While passing through Nebraska, I saw a *World-Herald*, and after reading about those gal wrestlers I have become very much interested. Could you send me some photos of the match between June Byers and Nell Stewart? What was the weight of June, and how would she stack up against Mildred Burke?"

One would certainly hope the editors of the *Evening World-Herald* obliged Corporal Dave Smith of Camp Atterbury, Indiana. The young soldier's correspondence is evidence that June was starting to turn heads all across the country while heading into her second year as a professional wrestler. No doubt many were beginning to ask the same question: could she be the one to defeat Mildred Burke?

Many women had tried and failed, though not as many as the public was led to believe. In the early days the pickings were slim, so Billy Wolfe booked sisters Mae Weston and Wilma Gordon, along with Elvira Snodgrass, under a variety of names in different cities. The new monikers made it seem as though Burke was knocking off one new challenger after another. In the pre-television, pre-Internet days of the 1930s, it wasn't hard to pull off.

The success of Burke and her rivals continued to attract new talent. Juanita Coffman and Mattie Bell were two of the many new opponents June Byers would face in 1946. Coffman, sometimes referred to as the Cherokee Tomahawk, was a nearly full-blooded Cherokee with jet black hair and 23-inch shoulders. She was a powerhouse at 180 pounds and known for using an airplane spin/slam as a finisher.

After a rough adolescence in an orphanage, Coffman was

spotted tearing tickets in a movie theater by a wrestling promoter who thought she had the right look and build. Coffman was a mainstay through the second half of the 1940s and one of the few ladies to have a couple of inches height over June Byers. She left the business at the age of 29 to marry wrestler Mike Gallagher and dedicated herself to being a wife and mother, but she always stayed in touch with many of her fellow wrestlers.

Mattie Bell, also a brunette, started training at the same time as Nell Stewart and was the reason Nell dyed her dark hair bleach blonde. The two women bore a striking resemblance to one another, and with good reason: they were sisters in real life. Bell would be ousted by Billy Wolfe from his women's wrestling organization after the two had a disagreement but not before becoming one of the few ladies to secure a win over both Nell Stewart and June Byers.

As Mildred Burke approached the decade mark in her celebrated reign, the fans who packed the smoke-filled arenas across the country speculated more and more, wondering who would be the one to finally end her undefeated streak.

United Press reporter named Jim Grieves became one of the first to profile June in January of 1946. As with many stories about "girl" wrestlers, some of the focus was on whether or not lady wrestlers lost their femininity, an idea June dismissed as "stuff and nonsense."

"I have met a good many of the women wrestlers and many are my best friends," said June. "They are for the most part educated and like to wear nice clothes like any girl. We make more money than working in restaurants or an office and can afford to buy nice clothes."

June also talked about her ambitions with Jim Grieves, specifically becoming the women's world champion. Missouri sports writer Gene Sullivan picked up the story in *St. Joseph News-Press* and declared her to be the woman most likely to dethrone Mildred Burke. "She has all of the natural ability required to reach the top," Sullivan wrote. "She lacks only experience."

Going into her second year, many promoters were already

speaking of June in the same sentence as Mildred Burke, often pitting her against another up-and-coming wrestler in a "winner gets a title shot" match to face Burke on a later date. In early 1946 June was always on the losing end of these contests. She was getting the experience, but she was doing so by putting other girls over.

She was also having a hellaciously good time, sometimes at the expense of people like Harry Cohen.

Poor Harry had seen better nights. Lying on his back in front of 5000 fans in the Kansas City Municipal Auditorium, he found himself locked between two powerful sets of legs trapped in a scissor hold.

It wasn't supposed to go this way. The girls were supposed to fight each other, not the official! Yet June Byers and Rose Evans seemed to keep coming back to him, knocking Cohen on his back and giving him the worst of it.

The only thing more fun than seeing a couple of wrestlers roughhouse an official was seeing two lady wrestlers do the same. June, dressed in blue satin, and Rose, wearing red, gave the crowd a riotous show abusing the 220 pound referee, yanking his hair and sending him flying around the ring.

Evans relished her role as the dirty villain during the January 8, 1946 contest. During the first fall, she tried to get June in trouble. "She's not supposed to gouge me in the eye!" she said, feigning injury. "She can't gouge me like that."

One fall later, it was Rose getting the stink eye from the fans. With Cohen on the mat, watching to see if June's shoulders were both touching, Rose would work one finger — and illegal hold — to try to get June to submit. Fans hollered for Cohen to catch Rose, but any time he looked up, she'd switch to the legal hold by grabbing all four fingers.

The scariest moment for June came in the third fall, as captured by a cameraman for *The Kansas City Times*. The newspaper ran a photo showing June with the top two ropes twisted around her neck. Rose was looking on smugly while Cohen attempted to free Byers from the ropes.

"A moment later, June was freed," said the caption, "And it was Cohen who was on his back."

Cohen ended up on his back thanks to June. After getting free, Byers managed to trap Rose's head between the ropes, delivering a series of kicks to the heel while prancing around the ring. After a kick intended for Evans hit Harry Cohen, June grabbed him by the hair and flipped him across the mat.

Two nights later in Columbia, Missouri, June found herself flying through the ropes into the laps of paying customers. Ann LaVerne took the heel role that night, repeatedly ignoring the referee's admonitions as she tossed June about like a rag doll. The ref tired of LaVerne's dirty work and awarded a victory to Byers, but the ladies managed to steal the show from a main event featuring Rose Evans and Nell Stewart.

June put in a little more referee abuse in Chattanooga on January 18 when she faced Nell Stewart in a singles match. After losing the first fall to Nell, June came back with a furious offense to win the second and third. Referee Howard Brown got a little too close to the action and lost his shirt to June's ripping and tearing. Once again, the ladies stole the show, outshining the men in front of 2000 fans.

Referee Clete Kauffman was the unsuspecting victim in a match between Nell and June that took place in Dayton, Ohio. Local columnist and unabashed lady wrestling fan Marj "Kid" Heyduck was on hand for *The Dayton Herald* to capture the moment as Nell, "in rose tights that hugged her curves better than any outfit Betty Grable ever wore," and June, wearing a suit of maroon satin with blue kid shoes, assaulted the ref with as much vigor as they did one another.

"Clete Kauffman figured in most of the grappling," Heyduck wrote to her "Boss," the sports editor. "He got his hair pulled out and his face pushed in. He got smacked to the mat."

No matter who the opponent, the ladies were almost certain to steal the show when they dropped the science of wrestling for good old fashioned brawling. On April Fool's Day in Portland, Maine, while tied at one fall a piece, June and Nell Stewart spilled out of the ring and traded the grappling for old fashioned fisticuffs inches away from the front row fans.

June made her debut in Alberta, Canada over the summer, a territory she would get to know well in the coming decades. In a rare negative review, a reporter for *The Lethbridge Herald* said the match between June and Rose Evans on July 15 left him strangely cold. "It was just plain silly and so obviously phony that it wasn't even amusing. The only astonishing thing was that there were spectators who actually got so worked up that they bellowed and bawled like calves who had lost their mothers. Some even ran to ringside, including a woman. It was amazing to see so many women among the spectators."

The *Lethbridge* journalist described the match as an act, and not a very good one. His attitude reflected many readers in Western Canada who were slow to warm to the idea of lady wrestling.

"How in heaven's name could anyone get himself or herself worked up over women wrestling is beyond me. If Monday night's wrestling match was a typical exhibition of the art, I'd have to be given a bonus to go to another one."

June and Mattie Bell received a much different welcome from the *Calgary Herald* after a contest on July 16 in Drumleller. "When it was said the female of the species was more deadly than the male, the writer must have had in mind women wrestlers."

Still playing the babyface, June made a young man's night in Portland one evening during a tag match with Juanita Coffman, Evelyn Wall, and Nell Stewart. In between matches, the fellow asked June to sign his autograph book. June smiled and said she would be delighted, taking the fan's notebook and signing her name. Then he made a mistake. He asked Juanita Coffman to sign the book. Coffman had been playing the heel that night, and the fans were so irritated with her, they booed the autograph seeker to the point he had to flee from ringside.

Such moments were both gratifying and frustrating. As much

as June enjoyed being a star and receiving the adulation of the fans, the heels were getting the wins because the babyface champion needed heel challengers.

It was difficult to stand out in the crowd, with more and more ladies coming aboard and working for Billy Wolfe. It quickly became apparent that you needed a hook or a gimmick to get ahead. Sister Nell Stewart succeeded in part because of her bleach blonde hair, while brunette sister Mattie Bell never quite broke through. Elvira Snodgrass's hillbilly routine set her apart as well, though she ultimately dropped the barefoot redneck act for the Hollywood glamour girl image.

In the spring of 1946, June tangled with veteran grappler Celia Blevins. Blevins was a full-blooded Native American from Oklahoma who started wrestling in 1941. A year later, a packed house at the Legion Arena in Pensacola, Florida became unusually quiet and solemn as Celia Blevins stepped into the ring with wrestler Jack LaRue and County Judge Harvey Page. Blevins and LaRue were legally wed that night, and the fans tossed so much rice into the ring at the conclusion of the nuptials, the mat had to be swept before LaRue could wrestle the main event with Jack Roller.

Ann Miller started working with June in the summer months. Miller told reporters she had been a night club singer prior to taking up the wrestling game. The opportunity to travel made wrestling attractive, and Miller was hopeful she and the other ladies would ultimately tour Europe once the war was over.

Helen Hild also joined June for the first of many matches that summer. Born Gladys Helen Nevins in 1926, Hild was sometimes booked as Gladys Galento and a frequent opponent of June Byers. In 1954 she had a son with singer Ted Wills whom she named after his father. She later married wrestler "Iron Mike" DiBiase, who adopted her son. June would play a role in assisting Helen's son pursue his dream, helping train young Ted DiBiase and start him on the path to becoming The Million Dollar Man.

On January 21, 1947, June participated in a very special

program that took place in Louisville, Kentucky. Throughout the 22 years that the Allen Athletic Club's ran shows in Louisville, the weekly wrestling program normally took place at the Columbia Gym on Fourth Street (now part of the Spalding University campus), but from the fall of 1946 to the fall of 1947, the company ran shows in the much larger Armory, a building later renamed Louisville Gardens.

The undercard of this special program saw Lou Thesz defeating Frankie Bockwinkel, Felix Minute defeating Ole Olson, and June Byers defeating Dot Dotson. But the star of the evening was a man who had never wrestled in Louisville before and never would again, 36-year-old Gil Woodworth from Florida.

Gil claimed to be a resident of the Florida Everglades and had come to wrestle another native of the South Florida swampland: a seven-foot alligator. Woodworth bragged to the *Courier-Journal* in a special interview that he had been declared a natural for wrangling alligators by alligator farmer Ross Allen of Silver Springs Florida Reptile Farm. He also boasted he had done some stunt work for Johnny Weissmuller in the *Tarzan* movies.

June defeated Dot in less than thirteen minutes. While Thesz was taking care of Bockwinkel and Woodworth his alligator, she freshened her hair and makeup and donned a dress for the night cap: a wrestling wedding.

Weddings were nothing new by this point in professional wrestling, as the story of Celia Blevins demonstrated. George Wagner, who later became Gorgeous George, was married numerous times around the country to his first wife. It was a great gimmick not only to draw a crowd but take home some extra gifts.

Justice of the Peace Herman Jorris was on hand to wed Gil Woodworth to Miss Perma Crook of Ripley, Tennessee before a crowd of 7300 fans. June stood at Miss Crook's side as her maid of honor. It was a memorable night for all, but especially promoter Heywood Allen, who netted $7300 at the gate. It would be his final event as co-owner of the Allen Athletic Club. A few weeks later, Allen revealed he had sold his interest to Francis and Betty McDonogh, his business partners from day one in 1935.

There's no indication that June Byers and the lovely bride had ever met before that night in Louisville, but her position in the wedding represented her current status in the wrestling business. She was a bridesmaid. So was Nell Stewart. So were Juanita Coffman, Ann Miller, Celia Blevins, and all the other ladies battling it out night after night.

Not that she was complaining of course. "I used to make $37 a week at an oil company," she told a Pittsburgh reporter. "I now average $7500 at this game."

June had already made it clear she was aiming for the championship, even saying she had no time for love until that goal was accomplished. Still, there was only one bride in the women's wrestling game. The heels at least got to dance with the bride.

In just two years, June Byers had criss-crossed the United States. She roamed the Eastern seaboard from Portland, Maine to Miami. She'd crossed the South, from Georgia to Texas to Arizona, up the Pacific Coast to Washington, roamed the prairies, the mountains, the Midwest, and even ventured into Canada.

"I used to average about 125,000 miles a year while wrestling between traveling by plane and car," Byers told Jim Melby in 1984. "I lived my life by minutes not hours. I had things down to a pretty good science of just how much time I had to leave for doing interviews, training, wrestling, etc."

Two years, thousands of miles, and yet in all her travels, she had not crossed paths with the reigning, defending women's champion. That was soon to change.

BLONDE BOMBSHELL

Dressed to kill, her blonde hair reset, her makeup flawless, June Byers grabbed her bag and headed for the rear entrance to the Music Hall in Cincinnati. All she wanted was to get some rest in the motel up the street before hopping in the car with her travel companions to work the next show in Canton.

Before she could even think about sleep, she had to deal with the inevitable: a handful of gentlemen assembled in the alley, waiting for a chance to meet June, Ann Laverne, Dot Dotson, or Evelyn Wall.

These men came prepared, bearing flowers, boxes of candy, and other emblems of affection. Chorus girls had dealt with the "problem" for decades, the Stage Door Johnnies hoping that the wink the lady with the long legs lobbed from the stage was more than just a show.

The lady wrestlers had them as well, gentlemen suitors hoping that the woman they just saw pummeling another into submission had a softer side.

"One of my biggest thrills was to walk in a dressing room and see it filled with flowers," Byers told Jim Melby in 1984. "Many people were kind enough to give me candy, but I really had to stay away from that, but I did eat all of the steaks and salad that I wanted. I do have many nice mementos from my career."

Some took full advantage of the moment. Others, including those who preferred the company of the same sex, accepted the gifts with a polite smile and a thank you. All of them enjoyed the attention, including June Byers.

"Sometimes it's a bother," Byers told *The Cincinnati Post* in 1947, "But being a woman, I sort of like the attention. The fellows who succeed in getting a formal introduction soon found that a lady wrestler is just that – a lady."

And what of the men who get a little too pushy? In 1950 June told writer Scott Baillie about a gentleman fan who followed her all the way from Birmingham to Albuquerque.

"How did you get rid of him?" Baillie asked. "With the crooked head scissors or maybe a front body throw?"

"Goodness no!" said June. "We're ladies just like anybody else. I called a cop."

Heading into 1947, June found herself back in the ring with two of the more senior ladies of the women's wrestling set, Mae Weston and Elvira Snodgrass. The three women worked matches across Texas as well as a Midwest loop that included Louisville, Evansville, and numerous towns across Ohio.

Helen Hild joined the girls on some of these shows, as did Dot Dotson and Evelyn Wall. Dotson and Wall were both fairly new to the business, and while Wall would not wrestle much beyond 1947, Dotson was just getting started. She entered the business after catching the eye of wrestling promoter Phil Duffy completely by accident. Duffy spotted a lady cab driver on the side of the road struggling with a much larger man. Thinking chivalrously, he pulled over and asked the woman if she needed help.

"No I don't," said Dot Dotson, as she dropped the man with a left hook.

Duffy stuck around long enough to see the bruiser hauled off by the police and hand the woman his business card. Dotson gave up the taxi for the wrestling ring and embarked on a career spanning more than twenty years.

Dot Dotson enjoyed another passion that June Byers would later have in common: a love of planes. The former cabbie loved flying so much, she claimed she was "supporting a plane" rather than supporting a husband, as some of the other women did.

Marj "Kid" Heyduck once again covered the action in Dayton, Ohio when Dot and June "took lady rassling out of the kick-bite-scratch league and put it up there with the men's style." Known as "The Woman in the Hat," she was one of the most beloved newspaper writers of her day and won more than seventy-five awards for her work. In her 33-year career, she rose from a staff writer on the women's page to editor of the women's page and ultimately assistant to the editor of the merged *Journal Herald*.

One of the greatest allies the ladies of the ring had, Heyduck enjoyed being a woman in a man's world any time *Dayton Herald* sports editor, whom she addressed in her columns as "Boss," gave her the nod to cover the local matches. She also featured many of the lady grapplers in her "Tea with Marj" column, inviting friends and foes to join her for tea and conversation prior to their matches in Dayton.

Kid Heyduck gave special attention to the more traditional action the ladies displayed, stealing the show from the likes of The Great Kirilenko, Wild Bill Zim, Ali Aliba, and Farmer Jones, who brought his pet possum to the ring. This was not a night of hair pulling and nail scratching. The girls worked hard, with June taking two out of three falls on a referee's decision after Dot refused to let the ref untangle June's head from the ropes.

"She might have spent less time in there had a woman, instead of a man, been the referee," suggested Kid Heyduck. "A male referee in a ladies's match always tries to act like a gentleman, Boss, and that's one character that's out of character then!

"How about campaigning for a lady ref the next time the lady rasslers come to town, Boss? She might not be a lady, but she'll know what the book says about socking another lady in the teeth!"

June was a big enough star by mid-1947, she received notice in *Quote*, an Indianapolis publication that compiled quotes from numerous sources into a weekly digest. Not surprisingly, June spoke about her chosen profession and her belief wrestling was for everyone, including women.

"If they'd only try," said June, "Women would find that wrestling gives them a delicate sense of balance, more self-confidence, and above all, really sound health."

Iowa wrestling legend Dan Gable, who once said, "Wrestling isn't for everyone, but it should be," would no doubt approve of June's sentiments.

Fans noticed in the newspaper ads promoting an appearance by June Byers in 1947. She was still dressing in the satin top with shorts, but the smile that had dazzled her coworkers now appeared in her promotional photos. Her hair was also noticeably lighter since going blonde, a change that would not stick for the long term.

Some fans also saw a change in June's wrestling style as the summer approached. While still playing the babyface in many arenas, she was doing more hair-pulling, more choking, more stomping, more rule-bending. The heel turn was inevitable, if June wanted to challenge for the women's world championship, and June proved she'd learned plenty from Mae Young, Elvira Snodgrass, Gladys Gillem, and Ann LaVerne about how to play dirty. She was more than ready to tangle with the queen of the ring. She only needed the opportunity.

The first clash between the current and future champions was scheduled to take place in the least likely of towns: Bowling Green, Kentucky. Located 65 miles north of Nashville, Tennessee and 119 miles south of Louisville, the town of Bowling Green enjoyed wrestling action presented by Bob Randall, who presided over the Southern Kentucky Wrestling Club. The 1947 season, which usually began in April, had been delayed, thanks to high winds that damaged the tent used to house the weekly wrestling shows during the summer months.

The tent finally opened for business on the corner of Kentucky and Eighth Street in May. Randall gave the fans a taste of women's wrestling in June with a match between Nell Stewart and Evelyn Wall, both "contenders" for Mildred Burke's title. Then in September, the queen herself was scheduled to make an appearance.

Bob Randall was certainly seeing dollar signs when the ink dried on the contract with Burke. The ad for the September 18 show in *The Park City Daily News* announced that no free passes would be issued "due to Miss Burke's contract." Yet as much as *The Park City Daily News* hyped the contest between Mildred Burke and June Byers, the single page of sports coverage in the September 19 paper did not give the results of the show.

While we may never know who won the Junior Heavyweight Championship between Herb Welch and Left "Atomic" Pacer, we know one thing for certain: June Byers did not wrestle Mildred Burke that night. She was in Algiers, Louisiana, where she defeated Dot Dotson for — what else? — a title shot against Mildred Burke on a date to be determined.

June returned to Dayton, Ohio in November, and Kid Heyduck was on hand to put the ladies over again when June, Juanita Banks, Dot Dotson, and Helen Hild stole the show in a tag match. "Six hundred pounds of curvaceous glamor — in four well-stacked packages — took over Memorial Hall last night," Heyduck penned in the November 26, 1947 edition of *The Dayton Herald*. "Averaging one black eye and 150 pounds each, the girls provided 35 minutes of fussin' that had some of the spectators apoplectic with commotion."

Heyduck made note of each lady's appearance: Dot wore black tights, maroon trunks, and a sullen expression. Helen Hild was dressed in green. June, still a blonde, was in baby blue satin and chewed gum throughout. Juanita Banks wore red and black and sported a burn on her left thigh: a "gift" from an irate Cincinnati fan who crossed the line and extinguished a cigarette on her leg a few nights before.

Once again, the ladies had the opportunity to put a man in his place. "The fans laughed longest and loudest when referee Jack Fisk got himself tangled in the arms and legs of four lady rasslers who can take care of themselves and any half-dozen referees with no trouble at all," wrote Kid Heyduck. "Oh well, Fisk'll probably recover in time."

In December June Byers went on a barnstorming tour with Violet Viann. As the daughter of Billy Wolfe and the sister of G. Bill, Violet would become June's sister-in-law for a very brief time in the 1950s.

Viann earned the nickname "The Cop Killer" from her father and the girls one night after a show in Columbus. While waiting for June to come out of the locker room, she lit up a cigarette, drawing the attention of one of the night watchmen. The watchmen ordered her to put the cigarette out and, for emphasis, gave her a shove.

Viann was holding June's diamonds in her purse at the time, and when the watchman shoved her, the rocks spilled out onto the floor. Viann got mad. She punched the man in the solar plexus and dropped him to his knees.

"I felt sorry for him," one of the ladies who witnessed the incident told New York reporter Earl Wilson. "It took eight cops to quiet her."

The contests June and Violet wrestled at the end of 1947 all came with a promise: the winner would get a title shot against Mildred Burke. Byers had wrestled many "winner faces Burke" matches, losing most and winning a handful, but the "dates to be determined" for her title shots never materialized. A week after her road trip with Violet Viann, the wait finally ended. June Byers, at last, would dance with the queen.

The Mildred Burke story bears much in common with that of June Byers. Both were young mothers when they turned to the wrestling game. Both were attracted by the lure of fame, fortune, and diamonds. Burke saw them dripping off Barbara Ware, the woman he would leave to marry Burke. Byers saw them on Burke and Billy Wolfe. Just as Burke wanted what Ware had, Byers had her eye on Burke's jewels, especially the ones around her waist.

The first clash between Mildred Burke and the woman who would eventually unseat her took place in front of a crowd of 5500. As June stepped into the ring with Mildred Burke on December 15, 1947 in Tulsa (OK) Coliseum for a two-out-of-three falls main event clash, she thought back to the diamonds Billy Wolfe wore the day she met him. The "lady" act Wolfe insisted all his ladies exude in public was not an act for June like it was for some of the girls. She wanted the finer things in life. She wanted diamonds, big cars, and fine clothes. She'd been afforded a taste of the good life in her three years in the business. But what if she could seize the title? What if she could unseat the champ and become the star attraction of the business?

It's unlikely June Byers could have "shot" on Mildred Burke and taken the title by force. It's also far less likely such a thought occurred to her in December of 1947. Shooting on the champ would not only lead to a humiliating loss at the hands of the smaller woman but a loss of income, maybe even a loss of her job. If you wanted to be a lady wrestler, you worked for Billy Wolfe. Mildred Burke was Billy Wolfe's champion. The woman who took Mildred Burke's title would do so when Billy chose and Millie allowed it. In theory.

June knew her role. Rile up the crowd. Put some doubt in their minds. Make them think maybe, just maybe, history might be made. Then put the champion over. Make Millie look as rich as the diamonds she wore when she wasn't in the ring.

Bend the knee. Bow to the queen.

June paid her dues. She lost to Mildred Burke on December 15 in Tulsa; December 16 in Little Rock, Arkansas; on December 17 in Springfield, Missouri; on December 18 in Joplin, Missouri; and on December 19 in Oklahoma City. Their swing through tornado alley completed, the two women headed home to enjoy the holiday.

It was just another week for Burke, another series of victories with a new challenger whose job was to reaffirm Burke's status. For Byers, it was much more. She'd tasted the ultimate spotlight, going toe to toe with a champion so firmly entrenched, her face was on the very golden belt she wore to the ring.

Byers wanted that gold, and like many of her contemporaries, she was willing to go to great lengths to get it.

WORKING STIFF

It's no secret that many of the women who got ahead in the age of Mildred Burke did so thanks to a close relationship with Billy Wolfe. The ink was barely dry on the marriage license between Burke and Wolfe before Wolfe was sleeping with some of his wife's co-workers.

Gladys Gillem admitted her affair with Wolfe openly in the documentary *Lipstick and Dynamite*. Understanding that sex with the boss could lead to better bookings which, in turn, led to better paydays, Gillem took full advantage. It wasn't about love, but then, neither was the marriage between Billy Wolfe and Mildred Burke.

Gillem's career and her relationship with Wolfe came to an end in the mid-1940s and coincided with the rise of Nell Stewart. At the same time he was crafting her into the Betty Grable of pro wrestling, Billy Wolfe was making her his favorite travel companion. Wolfe had enough women to split into two groups on the road, and when he wasn't traveling with his wife, he was sharing a bed with Nell Stewart. Just like Gillem before her, Nell's place on the wrestling cards improved thanks to her relationship with the boss.

Billy's philandering was no secret, not even to his wife. But one can hardly consider Mildred Burke a victim of a faithless husband. Burke's marriage was always primarily about business. Besides, Burke had her own long-term lover on the road: Billy Wolfe's son, G. Bill Wolfe.

It wasn't long before the rumors and whispers were circulating about June Byers as Nell Stewart. The rumors were fueled in part by a five-carat diamond ring that Byers began wearing on the road. Billy Wolfe loved diamonds and the status they conveyed. So did his wife. So did June. She often cited the diamonds she saw dripping off Burke as one of the reasons she took up wrestling.

Byers became one of Billy's lovers as well. She was single at the time, and again, the marriage between Wolfe and Burke was nothing more than a business contract. The relationship between Byers and Wolfe was likely all business as well.

"She was married 5 times," granddaughter Kay Parker says. "And once to Billy Wolfe's son. But she probably did do some things she wasn't proud of. Or even made to do. I hate to hear about it."

Sleeping with Billy Wolfe was no guarantee that a woman would get better bookings, but it clearly didn't hurt. It was incentive enough for many of the women he employed to do it. Those who were most successful, like Byers and Nell Stewart, earned the ire of many lady wrestlers. Byers in particular was vilified by some of her peers and many of Mildred Burke's most ardent fans over the years.

Regardless of what Byers did behind closed doors with the boss, the idea that she merely slept her way to the top is selling the woman short. Billy Wolfe granted favors for those who did him favors, but he still had a business to run. The women who worked the hardest sold the most tickets and rose to the top of the cards.

Few could claim to have worked harder than June, especially in-between matches. She loved to brag about her workout regimen.

"See these muscles?" she asked a reporter in St. Paul, Minnesota in 1962. "They are the muscles of a great athlete. They are long muscles, not short ones." She pulled up the sleeve of her sweater and exposed her calf to emphasize her point. "I've always lifted weights, but not heavy ones. I've worked on light weights and built my muscles by repetition not by heavy exercises."

One of the keys to her success, Byers claimed, was her dedication to working out. She would often spend four hours a day doing barbells, medicine balls, road work, parallel bars, and other apparatus to build muscle and endurance. She drank orange juice by the gallon and joked that the citrus drink made her sweat smell like orange blossoms.

June told her grandkids that she would ask her driver pull over and let her out on the side of the road. She'd run for a mile or so, her driver following at her pace, until she felt she had a good enough workout and got back in the car. June also preferred working a busy schedule. The more nights in a row she wrestled, the easier it was to keep in top ring shape and power through all those injuries.

In 1956 June told the *Nanaimo Daily News* in British Columbia that the working out never stopped, even in those rare instances when she took time off. "During this time, she doubles her exercises, and does them seven days a week. A full workout takes up to four hours of the Champ's time, plus gym workouts and five miles of running a day. 'Just the facts, ma'am. 'Jus the facts are enough to kill the average person."

And then, there's June's ring style.

There are differing philosophies on how wrestlers should work in the ring. While all wrestlers are trained on the same basics — the flat back bump, the collar and elbow lock up, going left for a headlock, using the left hand to whip someone into the ropes — they all vary in how they perform kicks and punches.

No one in professional wrestling throws their hardest punch or kick in the ring. At least, no one who wants to go on working in the business for more than a few matches. But some wrestlers are considered to be "stiffer" than others. They like to make it sting, and they expect their opponents to work stiff with them in return. The goal isn't to hurt their opponent, mind you. It's to be as real as possible by actually being real.

If we were to chart stiffness on a spectrum, it's a sure bet June Byers would be one of the stiffest wrestlers of all time. Certainly in the world of women's wrestling, she'd be on the extreme end when it comes to striking. Translated to today's wrestling scene, she would have felt right at home in the ring with Heidi Katrina, Shayna Baszler, and Asuka.

While researching Mildred Burke's biography, author Jeff Leen heard many stories from June's contemporaries about her penchant for working stiff. "While Nell Stewart was a pleasure to wrestle, June was always a terror. They said she had a wrist slap to the breastbone that really stung. This was a move that Billy Wolfe had used when he worked as a heel in the ring; maybe he taught it to her. Mae Young was dismissive of June's abilities when I interviewed her, but I chalked that up to sour grapes and envy and jealousy. June, after all, got the championship that Mae never did."

June's time in the ring with Elvira Snodgrass may have contributed to her toughness. The "Scufflin' Hillbilly" worked barefoot when she first adopted the Snodgrass name from her then husband Elmer Snodgrass. She loved to roughhouse, and when she was in character, no woman or man in the ring was safe. Elvira ripped the shirts off many a male referee, and she once confronted a fan in a hotel elevator after he attempted to lay hands on her during the show earlier that evening.

"If I'da got hold of you, I'da worked you over good," she said, surrounded by shocked bystanders. "Understand, I wouldn't have slugged you. Down at Smoky Mountain, Tennessee, where I come from, ladies don't hit gents. They just grab 'em and shake 'em 'til their nose bleeds."

Belle Starr laughed when asked about Elvira in 2022. She only met Elvira briefly, some time in the early 1950s, but the veteran left an impression. "She beat the hell out of me."

June proved to be cut from the same cloth. She'd trained with the boys in Houston, and she felt right at home with the hard hitting ladies of the ring. But not everyone appreciated June's smash mouth style, particularly the ladies who came in later years of her career.

"You had to give June Byers back what she delivered," said Ella Waldek in the 2004 documentary *Lipstick and Dynamite.*

"Wrestling Byers in huge coliseums or auditoriums, I knew exactly how Daniel in the Bible felt when he was thrown into the lion's den," said Penny Banner, who wrestled June well over a hundred times.

Banner described both June and Nell Stewart as artists, precise in their motions, never missing a move. Yet most preferred working with Nell, who was not only more of a charmer, but less likely to take your head off.

"She was excellent but she should have stayed with amateur wrestling where she could knock the hell out of you and get away with it and not have the competition she had," said Ella Waldek. "I used to see the girls she wrestled with and they'd come out of the ring looking like a piece of ground up hamburger. There was no reason for it. The girls were so in awe of her being one of the top people that they were afraid of doing anything that would get them fired. She skated by a lot. She was a very good wrestler, she was very athletic. She held in there. She held her own."

More than anything, Waldek hated the June Byers Slap. "There was no reason to be that vicious with that kind of slap. It didn't make sense. It wasn't a hold, and it didn't get a rise out of anybody. It wasn't fun. And there was no reason to do it."

Fans of Wahoo McDaniel, Ric Flair, independent star Cash Flo, and others would disagree Waldek's assertion that no one gets a rise out of a good hard chop.

"She did say she was the roughest in the ring," says granddaughter Kay Parker. "The other ladies would tell her, 'Easy girl. We have a whole match to wrestle through.'"

June became famous for one of the most unique finishing moves in the history of the sport, the Byers Bridge. There's footage of her applying the move to numerous opponents on YouTube, but the gist goes like this. With her opponent lying on her back, Byers faces away from her opponent, positioning her rival's legs straight up in the air, the backs of their knees lined up with her own. Byers then bends back into a bridge, her hands on the mat, her back to the woman's chest, her hair in the girl's face, holding her in place for a painful looking pin.

The closest comparison in modern wrestling is the Figure 8 used by Charlotte Flair who, coincidentally, almost played June Byers in a movie about Mildred Burke's life. Charlotte puts her father's

Figure 4 Leg Lock on her opponent and then goes into a bridge, away from her rival. June bent her foe backwards, bridging over the top of her, in a seemingly unbreakable hold.

"I actually developed the hold accidentally," she said in an interview with J. Michael Kenyon for the *WAWLI Papers* #579 (Wrestling As We Liked It). "During a match I grabbed an opponent's hands, they fell back with my legs in between, hooking them, I bridged back in a suplex for a winning pin, and that is how the hold was developed. Actually my opponent's momentum carried me backwards, so although I found a new hold and won a match, it happened in such a manner that I almost knocked my brains out doing it."

It's a maneuver as unique as the woman who created it.

"I used to be asked by the press why I wanted to be a wrestler," June Byers told Jim Melby. "I told them that I liked the money, minks, and diamonds. I also stressed the fact that they should feel my muscles, that I was for real. I not only got banged around, bled, and was injured, I had to spend time away on the road from my son, so I earned it the hard way."

Whatever June did behind closed doors, whatever her contemporaries may have felt about her style, there's no denying June worked hard. She sacrificed blood, sweat, tears, and time away from Billy Boy. She put in the hours every day to keep in shape. She put the miles on her cars and her body. She left everything in the ring, every night, and when it was done, she fixed her makeup, packed her bag, and drove to the next town to do it all over again.

BITING AND CLAWING

Mildred Burke didn't mind good competition. She welcomed it. Understanding that a champion is only as great as their rivals, Burke loved when a new challenger emerged. It made the box office fresh. It gave the fans something new, a dangerous new threat who may have what it takes to unseat the long-reigning champion.

Burke also understood that many of the young ladies rising up to challenge her had a chip on their shoulder. Billy Wolfe kept his wife isolated from the other women as much as he could, shielding his affairs from his wife and fueling the resentment the challengers had towards his champion.

Burke could sense the hunger, the desire in each new challenger who stepped in the ring. She knew the ultimate goal of each girl was to take her spot, yet she remained supremely confident. She knew Billy Wolfe had no one who could draw like she did, and she knew she could handle any challenger who dared to shoot on her.

The first challenge from June Byers had come and gone. Burke would take it easy to start 1948 while June Byers traveled the back roads of her home state, working singles and tags while traveling with Juanita Coffman, Helen Hild, and Dot Dotson. In February she and Dot Dotson headed north to travel with Ann Miller and Violet Viann. June also saw action with Theresa Theis, a teenage rookie introduced to the sport by former Chicago Bears legend Bronko Nagurski. She later married wrestler Ray Stevens.

Despite her fall from the championship picture, Byers was winning almost every night. The Burke matches gave promoters another laurel to hang on her name while promoting their events, and her booking remained strong. Even on the nights she did lose, she kept her heat thanks to her position as the heel. If she was undone, it was

43

due to her own arrogance, or a referee bold enough to punish her misdeeds.

The Sidney Telegraph covered the action when June wrestled Helen Hild in Sidney, Nebraska on Match 25, 1948. Helen, working as Gladys Galento, wore yellow and took the babyface role while June, in purple, played the heel. Entering to thunderous applause and stomping feet, the ladies got right to work, forgetting about theory hair-dos and putting on "an acrobatic performance that was a joy to behold."

Hild took the upper hand early, but June seized the momentum when she locked Hild's neck in the ropes. The referee struggled to set Hild free, taking a few walloping kicks in the back from Byers in the process. June scored the first pin fall, and the ladies returned to the locker rooms for a brief pause.

When they came back to the ring, their hair had been reset, and their makeup fixed. They quickly went to work, messing both. Helen found an advantage by working the small of June's back, but June countered by throwing her rival out of the ring twice. Hild came in the second time with a head of steam and flattened Byers for the pin, tying the match at one a piece.

Hild and Byers didn't bother with hair and makeup prior to the third fall, by far the nastiest of all. In addition to the hair pulling and grappling, the fans saw plenty of biting. Byers bit Hild. Hild bit Byers. Byers bit the referee. Hild left the fans with a smile on their face, scoring the deciding fall and sealing the victory.

June worked just a few days in April 1948, a rare break in the schedule that indicates she could have been out nursing an injury. The girls, like the men, often worked hurt, afraid to lose their spot to someone new. This had been less of a threat for the ladies just a few years earlier, but with so many new girls coming on in the late 1940s, it was all the more imperative June didn't miss too many dates.

Throughout the course of her career, June Byers suffered her fair share of broken bones. "In the first nine years alone in the ring I broke ribs, both of my collarbones, my left arm, and many concussions," Byers told Jim Melby in 1984. "After some bouts I was so black and blue that I looked like a leopard. One time in El Paso, Texas I was impaled on a chair, and as a result, I had to have my gall bladder and appendix removed. In addition, every bone in my hands has been broken or fractured at one time. Thankfully I always healed fast, certainly working out constantly helped my body to restore itself."

June traveled to New England in May, where she locked up with Mildred Burke at the venerable Boston Gardens. The women's match was a co-main event alongside a man's title match featuring "Heavyweight Champion" Frank Sexton and European Champion Frederich von Schacht. Boston favorite Wild Bull Curry was also on the card, scheduled for a contest against The Great Mephisto.

More than 10,000 fans turned out for a show, and despite the championship pedigrees of Sexton and Von Schacht, all eyes were on the ladies. The coverage favored the ladies especially. The eight paragraph write up on May 7 spent six paragraphs on the ladies, one on the Sexton-Von Schacht match, and one on the two preliminaries, including Bull Curry vs. The Great Mephisto.

Burke dazzled in her white boots and white ring attire that included a pink, floral design on the right leg. Her hair was perfectly quaffed, her lips and nails a matching red. June wore black ring gear with black boots trimmed in gold. They looked like two friends prepared to take a summer stroll on the boardwalk. Then the bell rang, and any illusion the two were friends went out the door. Referee Steve Passas knew he had his hands full when he heard Burke scream as Byers took a huge bite of her leg during a scrum on the mat. Burke hurled a few nasty words at Byers, which *The Boston Globe* reduced to, "You so and so!" before taking a bite of one of June's fingers.

The *Globe* reporter acknowledged that, at times, the ladies seemed to be working in a manner to protect themselves from harm. Nevertheless, there was nothing fake about the bump June took out of the ring near the end. Taking a punch from Burke, June sailed across the gap between the ring and the spectators, crashing into the seats right in front of Cambridge police chief Ted Leahy. "There was nothing phony about this crash, and the wonder of it all was she wasn't hurt."

June spent most of May traveling the East Coast with Juanita Coffman, Elvira Snodgrass, and Mae Weston. Late in the month she started a loop from Ohio to Tennessee crossing paths with Mae Young, Helen Hild, and Theresa Theis along with Rose Evans and Elvira Snodgrass. May literally gave way to June on May 31 in Sandusky, Ohio when Mae Young lost a singles match to June two falls to one. The pun-loving beat reporter for *The Sandusky Register* took great delight handing in a story with the headline "Last Night Was End of May."

A Knoxville promoter took a bold step that summer while promoting an appearance from June Byers. *The Knoxville Journal* ran a promotional piece on June 20 under the headline "Only Foe To Defeat Burke Appears At Lyric Friday," claiming that June had recently defeated Mildred Burke in Kansas City. A follow up the next day noted that Burke had won a rematch a week later while also stating that Byers and her Knoxville foe, Juanita Coffman, had incited a riot during their previous clash in St. Louis.

There's no word in the Saturday edition of the *Journal* if Coffman and Byers lived up to their hype and incited a riot in Tennessee. The wrestling results were not printed in the Saturday edition, and with good reason. The paper devoted almost the entire page to boxer Joe Louis, who announced his retirement as champion after knocking out Jersey Joe Walcott in the eleventh round.

THE MONTREAL COVER-UP

Few cities have had as rich a history and as much controversy as Montreal, Quebec when it comes to pro wrestling. The city that gave the world Yvon Robert, Brute Bernard, Jos LeDuc, Pat Patterson, Jacques Rougeau, the Vachon family, Kevin Owens, Sami Zayn, Maryse Ouelet, Crazzy Steve, and LuFisto also gave us the 1997 Montreal Screwjob, where Vince McMahon ordered referee Earl Hebner to ring the bell and award the WWF World Heavyweight Championship to Shawn Michaels, even though the champ, Canadian icon Bret Hart, had not tapped out.

Wrestling history buffs and members of the Cult of (Jim) Cornette know well that the first Montreal Screwjob, originally known as the Battle of the Bite, took place back on May 4, 1931. Champion Ed "Strangler" Lewis was the victim this time. As planned, Strangler dropped the first pin fall, expecting to win the second and third, but during the second, DeGlane started screaming, claiming the champ had bitten his arm. The bite marks were real but had been created during the intermission by DeGlane or one of his compatriots in the locker room and concealed until the action resumed. The referee awarded the second fall to DeGlane in a scheme orchestrated by Strangler's business rival, Boston promoter Paul Bowser.

In 1948 June Byers and Rose Evans made some controversial history of their own just outside Montreal. The dust up began when a singles match between the two ladies was announced for a July 26 show at Verdun Auditorium, located in the borough of Verdun. Adrien Valiquette began promoting in the mid-1930s, and except for a brief time during World War II, had run shows in the town ever since. It would be the first ever presentation of women's wrestling in the city, and the fans were ecstatic.

The local government was not. Neither were the local churches. Women's wrestling was forbidden in the city of Montreal, but the law, as written, did not include Verdun. As soon as news broke about the women's wrestling match, civic and church leaders voiced their opposition. The idea of women wrestling was obscene and vulgar to many, especially given the semi-revealing costumes the ladies wore.

Alas there was nothing legally the forces that conspired against Byers and Evans could do. Women's wrestling was illegal in many places at the time, most notably in the State of New York. But the athletic commission that dictated the rules in Montreal had no jurisdiction over Verdun.

Unable to stop the match, Verdun Police Director Pierre Gatineau forced one change on the proceedings. He couldn't stop the match, but he ordered the two women to wear slacks and sweatshirts over their ring attire.

June Byers and Rose Evans clearly didn't care that they had detractors in the Montreal community. The English language edition of *The Gazette* from Montreal describes a scene as wild and outrageous as any match either woman ever put on. They were not about to pack it in, nor would they tame their actions in the ring. The ladies made their traditional entrances in their robes: June dressed in gold, Rose in blue. They disrobed, revealing the slacks and sweatshirts required by Director Gatineau. As a sold our crowd of 5500 looked on, the ladies waited patiently for referee Alex Paquette to ring the bell.

And then, the girls did what they did best.

Rose Evans began by yanking June around by the hair, gouging her eyes, and punching her right in the solar plexus.

Referee Paquette cried out, "Enough!"

Rose responded with a word of her own: "Scram!" And punched Paquette in the neck.

For nine minutes and fifty seconds, Rose Evans established herself as the heavy, brutalizing June from one side of the ring to the other.

"Good heavens!" cried a man in the front row, taken aback by the brutality.

Reluctantly, Paquette counted three as Rose Evans pinned June Byers. Fans booed as Paquette raised Rose's hand in victory, and the ladies retired to the locker rooms for a short break.

June freshened up her appearance before returning to the ring. Almost immediately, Evans put June flat on her back, but a tug at Rose's hair swung the momentum. The crowd cheered, and Referee Paquette struggled to hide his satisfaction as Byers hoisted Evans up, draped her over the ropes, and delivered a spanking.

Evans called Byers a "witch." At least, that's the word published in *The Gazette*. Paquette warned Evans about her language. Evans pulled Byers back to the mat by the arm, but Byers managed a reversal, allowing Paquette to count three and even the contest at one fall a piece.

The crowd was on their feet for the third and final fall. Rose Evans pulled out all the stops in the third, gouging June's eye and wrapping her neck in the ropes.

"Please, ladies, please!" Referee Paquette pleaded.

"Go hem-stitch a hanky!" Rose screamed.

June refused to quit. Calling on "everything she had ever learned about steer stumping in Texas," she threw Rose Evans to the mat, where she stayed long enough for the final three count.

"It was a perfect night for wrestling," Ron Marsh of *The Gazette* proclaimed. "Not only did the fragrance of peanuts and perspiration permeate the premises, but just inside the lobby a young man was cooking popcorn. Sometimes the crunching of the spectators was louder than the crunching of Miss Byers and Miss Evans. All the scene needed was Nero, lolling in a ringside seat, plucking his violin."

Mr. Marsh's recap appeared on page eleven beneath a photo that captured the moment when June spanked Rose while draped over the ropes. One can only imagine how thrilled local leaders and clergy were seeing Rose's *derrière* prominently featured in their morning paper.

"It was the first women's match in the province of Quebec," confirms Pat Laprade, who co-authored the outstanding book *Mad Dogs, Midgets and Screw Jobs: The Untold Story of how Montreal Shaped the World of Wrestling* with Bertrand Hébert. "Verdun was a separate town than Montreal, so the rules of the Athletic Commission didn't apply there. That's why in the 1970s Vivian Vachon was able to work in Verdun for Grand Prix but not at the Montreal Forum."

It would be thirty-seven years before a women's match actually took place in the city of Montreal in 1985.

Fifty three years after the Byers-Evans bout, in neighboring Ontario, a Montreal native named Genevieve Goulet, better known to indie fans everywhere as LuFisto, fought for the right not merely to wrestle, but to wrestle men in intergender contests. LuFisto had struggled her entire career to earn not just acceptance but respect in a business largely dominated by men. Like June Byers and Rose Evans before her, she broke ground and blazed a trail for herself and future generations.

An early promotional ad, sans smile, from February 1947 in Houston.

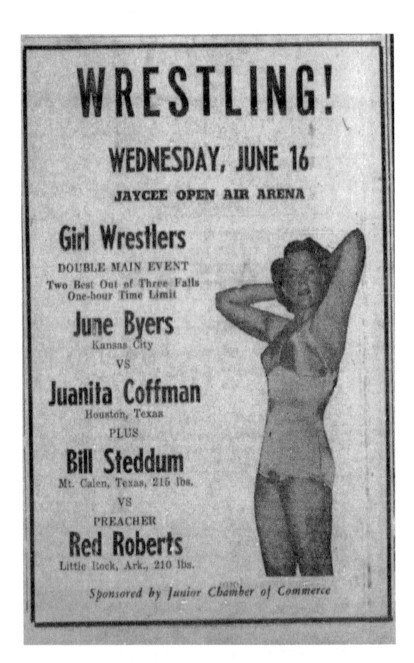

Missouri newspaper ad 1948.

A serious promo photo, sans smile.

A rough pair of rivals: Ann Laverne in the robe and Elvira Snodgrass in the cape.

On the cover of the program in Columbus, Ohio, in 1949.

WORLD'S GREATEST WRESTLERS

MILDRED BURKE - World's Woman Champion
Atomic MERCER - World's Fastest Wrestler
GENE (Mr. America) STANLEE
TELEVISION FAVORITE

Paterson Armory
Paterson, N. J.

Wed. Evening, May 18, 1949
8:45 P. M.

"Again A Hearty Welcome To All"

I appreciate the support given my first show April 8. My ambition has been to give the fans of Paterson and vicinity the best talent available. This second show has a champion in every bout. I sincerely hope you enjoy the matches. Please feel free to make suggestions. For information on future wrestling shows in Paterson, fill in the form on back page.

C. TURC DUNCAN
Promoter

MILDRED BURKE - 139
World's Champion Lady Wrestler
Los Angeles, California

JUNE BYERS - 145
(Texas Tornado) Contender
Houston, Texas

Early clash with the champ. Burke kept the title, but June's photo was larger.

Battling Theresa Theis in Philadelphia in 1949.

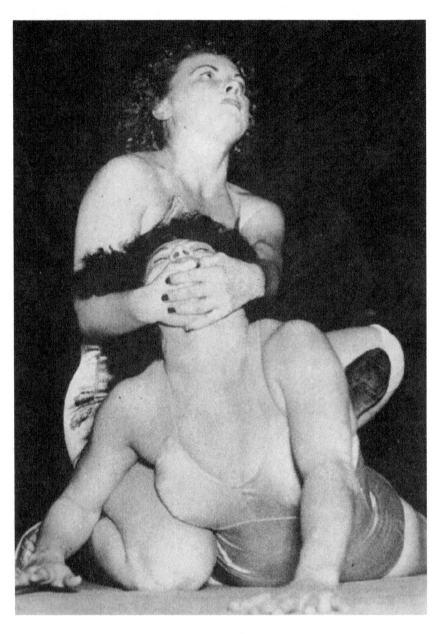

Working Mae Weston in Highland Park, NJ, 1949.

Same match in Highland Park.

Tangled up in the ropes in Highland Park, NJ, 1949.

Cincinnati television ad from 1950.

JUNE BYERS — GIRL WRESTLER

THE TEXAS TORNADO

"Where's the money?"

June Byers rooted through her purse a second time, and then a third. She asked the others at the table to check their purses and pocket books. The ladies didn't have it. Neither did the fellas.

The group entrusted June with holding on to their earnings for the night: $300 in all. She'd placed the cash in her bag. Now, sitting in a diner with a dinner check due, the money was gone.

Some got up to search the restaurant. One went out to look in the car. Frustrated, the group started to pitch in from the cash they hand on hand, paying the waitress so they could race back to the Coliseum in Opelousas, Louisiana.

They managed to get into the Coliseum, but the search turned up nothing. Three hundred dollars was a good chunk of change, almost $4000 in 2023 dollars. Everyone wanted their share so they could buy gas and food to get to the next town.

"What about the tavern?" someone suggested.

Of course! Before hitting the diner, they'd stopped at a little bar in Lafayette to have a drink. They drove back to the tavern, and June raced inside, asking if anyone had seen a small purse full of money.

The owner of the establishment smiled warmly. "Of course. We've been waiting for you." He handed the cash back to June, who thanked him profusely. She returned to the car to distribute the cash to a very relieved group of wrestlers.

The August 1948 incident in Cajun country reveals a rarely seen side of life on the road. Men and women of the mat were reliant on the pay from the promoters not just for making a living, but to get them to the next town. One missed pay day, one cheating promoter, or one lost purse could put a serious damper on a road trip.

Many of the wrestlers had family to think of, like June's son Billy. Having suffered through at least some of the depression, most knew how far a dollar and even a penny could stretch. A loaf of bread and bologna could feed a car full of money-conscious wrestlers for days on end.

Not that any of them were willing to portray themselves as skin-flints and tight wads before the general public — especially not the ladies! They worked hard to keep up appearances, not only making sure their hair and makeup was perfect but dressing in the latest fashions while on the road and extravagant ring attire during shows.

June turned heads in Atlanta when she walked to the ring dressed in "a heavy silver skirt, topped with turquoise satin bodice and sequin-trimmed cuffs, the whole thing lined with fuchsia satin," as described in the August 26, 1948 edition of *The Atlanta Constitution*. Miss Byers looked so ravishing in her entrance gear, the fans were sad to see her remove it prior to entering battle.

Byers told the *Constitution* that she designed her own gear and has a trunkful at home. "Moreover, she has a passion for dainty lingerie, dressy gowns, fur coats, and diamonds, and one of her real fears is she will be caught out in public with her fingernail polish chipped."

Such extravagance was expected of the ladies, especially those climbing up the cards and appearing in the main event. No longer content with the colored satin trunks and shorts she wore in her early days, June commissioned ring gear and robes designed to dazzle and impress from the moment she entered the arena. She was purchasing as many as five new outfits a year at a price range of $1000-1500, and her wardrobe drew favorable comparisons to Gorgeous George.

A contrast to this spending can be found in the ledger books left behind by "The Black Panther" Jim Mitchell, one of the most popular male stars of the era and a trailblazing African American. Mitchell recorded all his expenses from 1944 through 1949 in a little black book and spent, on average, $14 for "wrestling clothes" every few months. If he splurged and bought a robe to go with those trunks, he might spend as much as $60.

In the fall of 1948 June wrestled Lillian Ellison, a green rookie from South Carolina with her own dreams of money and diamonds. Within a few years, she'd adopt a new nickname, Slave Girl Moolah, which later morphed into The Fabulous Moolah. Byers worked a handful of matches with Ellison in September, whipping her in Harrisburg, Illinois; Louisville, Kentucky; and Evansville, Indiana.

A more formidable and unique competitor faced June for the first time a week after the matches with Ellison. Cincinnati girl Ada Ash was more than just a professional wrestler. She was a bodybuilder and a powerhouse, known for using the move Claudio Castagnoli fans refer to as The Big Swing.

Ada and her husband Al Szasz, also a wrestler, were known for their bizarre and breathtaking feats of strength. A photo of the couple shows Ada in a bridge position, on all fours with her belly up, supporting a small stack of concrete blocks. Al stood by his wife holding a sledgehammer, preparing to break right through the concrete resting on his wife's stomach. Ada and Al were also animal trainers, with some of their animals specializing in the combat arts. Both wrestled alligators and bears, and their trained kangaroo was a boxer.

Mildred Burke notched a few more wins on June in October, starting in Denver and winding up in Tennessee. She took two straight falls on "Shriner's Night" in Memphis before a crowd of 6000 fans in the Auditorium. The following evening in Nashville, the third largest crowd ever to attend a wrestling show in that town saw June take the first fall but lose the second and third.

Byers won several matches in a row from Mae Young after her third go-round with Burke before setting out on the road with Dot Dotson, Juanita Coffman, Helen Hild, and Theresa Theis, who was now a year into the business but still being introduced as an eighteen-year-old. Win or lose, June was working in front of packed houses, and always in the semi-main or main event. 4300 saw Burke defeat Mae Young in Des Moines in November. 7000 witnessed Dot Dotson's win over June in January.

In Dayton's Memorial Hall on December 7, one of the undercard matches featured a blonde, curly-haired former merchant marine in black trunks named Tug Carlson. A brilliant artist who was offered a scholarship to the prestigious San Francisco School for the Arts at the age of nine, Carlson was the very definition of the generic, "white meat babyface" of his day.

Like many male wrestlers who struggled to get noticed when billed beneath the ladies, he was growing frustrated. As good a hand as he was, Carlson knew he needed to evolve or he'd soon be out of a job.

June's public image continued to evolve. The scowl had disappeared completely from her press photos by 1949. Her winning smile now graced programs and newspaper ads everywhere she went, and her gowns became ever more elaborate. It's interesting to note that when she and Mildred Burke wrestled in Paterson, New Jersey on May 18, the photo of June in her robe was much larger than the one of Burke in her zebra-striped bikini.

June's love of dogs and horses became part of the promotional story. "She has raised Scottish Collies which have won many blue ribbons," proclaimed *The Sun Journal* of Lewiston Maine, "and is good enough on horseback to have taken part in a number of rodeos back in her home state of Texas." Newspapers and promoters were starting to pick up her new nickname: June Byers had become the Texas Tornado.

It was Paterson promoter Turc Duncan who proclaimed that after 6,000 years of male dominance, ladies were now out-drawing the men in the wrestling game. Duncan put his money where his mouth was, booking June for appearances in April and May. After June vanquished Juanita Coffman during her April appearance, Duncan achieved the "herculean task" of scheduling a match between Byers and the champ.

Burke and Byers faced off several times that spring, starting in Camden, New Jersey on April 11. Byers drew comparisons to the infamous Dusek Brothers in winning the first fall, setting Burke up for the comeback victory as she won the second and third. A crowd of 2700 was on hand to see Burke retain her undefeated record in Camden.

The match was much shorter when the ladies wrestled the next night in Baltimore for a Cancer Benefit Show on April 12. The ladies took a back seat to a main event featuring former world champion Jim Londos and Baron Michele Leone. Mildred Burke still won, finishing June Byers in fifteen minutes with an alligator clutch.

The ladies were back in the main event on April 14 in New Brunswick. Only 844 were in attendance, but Byers and Burke put on a show. June riled the crowd up by throwing Burke outside the ring, and the diminutive champion carried the fans on her back as she staged her comeback.

Boston hosted Burke and Byers for the second time on May 12. Sports reporter Jerry Nason of *The Boston Globe* hyped the fans for the occasion with some typical behind the scenes gossip for the times. "June raises show dogs and is cah-ray-zee about puppies. Millie is a great hand in the kitchen, majoring in banana cream pies. Referee Steve Pappas, nevertheless, is the nomination for The-Man-I-Most-Wouldn't-Like-to-Be-Tonight."

The crowd was smaller for the return match, but 5000 fans got their money's worth. June drew blood early on, punching Burke in the left eye and opening up a cut she'd sustained in a car accident. Burke got the win in two straight falls, working just over fifteen minutes total.

Turc Duncan's effort to book the ladies on May 18 paid off. A crowd of 4000 paid $5401.50 at the gate to see the Texas Tornado tackle the champ. Burke won again in straight falls, but the Paterson crowd got an extra seven minutes of action compared to the 5000 at the Arena in Boston.

GLAMOUR GIRL

"I was always a real fan, a fanatic after I saw my first wrestling match." Dressed in a gray faille suit and ankle strapped shoes, June Byers told her life's story to a reporter for the *Richmond Times-Dispatch* prior to an appearance in August of 1949. She spoke about leaving her job in a lab, and leaving her son at home with her mother, to travel more than 500,000 miles across North America in her Chrysler.

The rigors of the road left little time for hobbies, but June copped to having a few. She enjoyed sports and going to the movies, but mostly, she enjoyed collecting furs and diamonds.

"This one on my left hand has sixteen carats in it," she said, flashing the ring for the googly-eyed reporter. "This one on the right hand has four carats... and the one on my right pinkie has a two carat canary diamond and a two carat white diamond, all absolutely perfect." Byers was also wearing a diamond locket and diamond earrings. All told, the carat count came to thirty-three.

Ohio's *Columbus Sports Week Magazine* also took note of June's sparkling appearance. A March 18, 1949 story began with this scene from a local jeweler:

"There goes June Byers, the girl wrestler!"

The other girl said, "Are you kidding?"

The first girl who had identified June had good enough proof.

She and her boyfriend the day before had been in a downtown jewelry store looking over rings.

At the next counter was a pretty and well-dressed young lady in a fur coat who was purchasing a large diamond — and putting the cash on the line.

After she left, the salesman told the couple who she was.

June is a collector of diamonds and fur coats, and incidentally the coat she was wearing in the jewelry store cost $1500, and that's not peanuts, junior.

June was starting to look every bit the star and celebrity as Mildred Burke.

June had become an attraction in her own right. The fans had grown enamored with her ring gear that now rivaled the champ. She'd kicked the bleach blonde locks to the curb in favor of her own natural auburn color.

A pair of photos showing June apply a rear chin lock and delivering a devastating dropkick to Mae Weston appeared in papers all across the country during the spring of 1949, even in towns where Byers was not scheduled to appear. Whether she was a heel or face, whether she wrestled a veteran in Mae Weston or a teenage upstart like Theresa Theis, the Texas Tornado had a name that put butts into seats.

The same can be said for a twenty-five-year-old competitor now nicknamed The Rooster. "She pecks and claws at her mat opponents," said *The Richmond News Leader* on August 18, 1949, "And it wasn't long before wrestling fans had named her properly." You won't see mention of it in her biography, but it was none other than Lillian Ellison who embraced the barnyard moniker by sewing the image of a rooster onto her robes.

The woman who would become Moolah scored a few victories over June Byers as they traveled Virginia, North Carolina, and Ellison's home state of South Carolina. But this was 1949. Moolah was not yet Fabulous, and June was not yet a world champion.

While becoming the champ remained her primary goal, June was already talking about life beyond the ring. She wanted to become a promoter.

"You can say that my five years in wrestling have been a good course in promotion work," June declared. "When I'm not in action I can do a ballyhoo job as well as an expert."

The story of June's promotional ambitions was typed and distributed by the offices of none other than Billy Wolfe, and the interview ran in numerous papers across the country. "I'd like to promote wrestling in major stadiums or arenas, such as the Chicago stadium, Detroit arena, as well as Madison Square Garden," added June.

June went on the road with Mildred Burke in December of 1949, and Burke finished the year reminding Byers of her place. The champ and challenger linked up in chilly Casper, Wyoming and battled their way south through Denver, Colorado Springs, El Paso, and Albuquerque.

"The main event was by no means a lady-like affair," *The El Paso Times* recorded after the December 20 battle. Byers won the first fall, as she had many nights, and left the champion dazed after tossing her out of the ring. Dazed or not, Burke clamped Byers into a finishing hold and secured the inevitable victory.

June and Dot Dotson made the papers all across the country, thanks to a comment by wrestling promoter and boxing icon Mushky Jackson. One of the most colorful characters in the fight game, Jackson was considered a mastermind when it came to preparing a boxer for a big fight. He was equally well-known, and in some circles beloved, for his ability to mangle the English language in a fashion that makes Yankees legend Yogi Berra sound darn near intelligible.

"I got a good story for you about my heavyweight sometime," Mushky was heard to say walking into the 20th Century Sporting Club in New York one afternoon. "He's just out of the army and has placed himself under my tootage, or is that the word?"

Mushky booked the two ladies for a contest to be held at the Matawan-Keyport Rec Center in Matawan, New Jersey on January 18. So proud was Mushky of the main event promised to the New Jersey fans, he told the press, "In the mat world this pair has plenty of grunt-groans and will be a lively bout among the female sex." The mangled proclamation went out over the wire, making sports columns in more than a dozen states.

When June tackled Dot Dotson in Camden, New Jersey on a January night, she shook hands with a familiar face now going by a different name. In an effort to extend his career, Tug Carlson took a cue from Gorgeous George and Lord Patrick Lansdowne, donning flowing robes the ladies would have envied and reinventing himself as the haughty British nobleman Lord Leslie Carlton.

Carlton, whose real name was Leo Whippern, was in truth descended from Hungarian royalty. His British accent was terrible but just good enough to help him get heat from the fans. When his daughter asked him years later why he didn't make himself a German noble, a much easier sell, his answer reflected the temper of the post-World War II era: "I wanted them to hate me, not kill me." Hated as he was, Lord Carlton became a much bigger star than Tug Carlson ever could!

The fans in Trenton, Ohio got a show on February 5, when June and Violet Viann spent as much time pummeling the ref as one another. Byers used Bones Lionberger as a human shield early on after Viann got angry, and in the struggle to hide from Viann, June ripped the shirt off his back.

Bones brought more abuse on himself later in the contest when he shoved one of the women to force a separation. This time both June and Violet attacked Bones with their fists, striking him in the chest and shoulders.

New York columnist Earl Wilson got as close to feeling a punch from June Byers as he cared to get. While hanging out backstage with June, Mae Weston, Violet Viann, Dot Dotson, and Billy Wolfe, Wolfe asked Dot if she'd take a shot across the chest from June as a demonstration. Dot readied herself, standing flat-backed against, the wall, while June removed the diamonds from her left hand.

WHAP!

Wilson winced as he saw the blow delivered close up. Dotson looked over at the writer.

"Hurt?" he asked.

"It didn't feel good," Dotson groaned.

Violet Viann put on her best TV announcer voice. "Dotty's chest happens to be a little black and blue right now." The comment sent the girls into laughter, which grew even more intense when someone mentioned that Nell Stewart had punched out two of Mae Young's teeth a few nights earlier in the Carolinas.

Wilson looked over to see June rubbing her hand. "See? I got a swollen knuckle."

The ladies began to share their injury stories with Wilson. "I broke my clavicle til the bone came through the top," said Mae Weston.

Wilson shivered. "Is it worth all that?"

"Sure," said Viann. "It's worth it if you don't have to work 8 or 9 hours a day for $25 a week and have a boss over you every minute. You travel and get to see the country and you get $200 to $500 a week."

It's one thing to see the country through the windows of a car, passing one town after another. It's a different thing to experience the people, the culture, and events that make a place special. June was one of the fortunate few to experience the one sporting event that Louisville fans loved even more than wrestling: the Kentucky Derby.

June was booked in Louisville, Kentucky the first of May for two shows hosted by the Allen Athletic Club. Her opponent for the regular Tuesday night affair at the Columbia Gym was a woman who bucked the requirements set by Billy Wolfe for new applicants. Wolfe was looking for women who were single, fit, and photogenic; aged eighteen to twenty-four; weight between 130 and 150 pounds; no shorter than 5'2" and no taller than 5'7".

In other words, no smaller than Mildred Burke, and no bigger than June Byers.

Mars Bennett fit all of the above save for the age limit. She was 27 years old, but her beauty, athleticism, and charisma was undeniable.

It didn't hurt that she bore an uncanny resemblance to another muscular grappler, Mildred Burke.

Mars hated her birth name, Maude Audrey Foreit, and had it changed legally as soon as she was old enough. The Michigan native was a standout athlete in high school and worked as a riveter on B-24 bombers during World War II. After becoming a daring performer in the Clyde Beatty and Ringling Brothers and Barnum & Bailey Circuses, she became a popular subject for the cheesecake magazines and a favorite of men who liked their girls with muscles. If she wasn't demonstrating feats of strength, like lifting her male strength coach over her shoulders in a fireman's carry, she was either wearing boxing gloves or demonstrating various grappling holds. Wolfe gladly waived the age requirement when he saw Mars had the total package.

Mars and June battled to a draw on the Tuesday night show, so promoter Francis McDonogh booked them for a rematch on the Friday night Kentucky Derby Eve show.

Stealing the show would prove to be a challenge on Friday. The ladies had some unusual competition in that department, and not from the boys. Another lady, weighing 500 pounds, was scheduled to tackle the tag team of Floyd Bird and Pete Peterson: Ginger the Wrestling Bear.

Mars and June did their best to thrill the fans, with Mars using a dropkick to secure victory. Pete Peterson and Floyd Bird, of course, came up short in their efforts to pin Ginger. You have to admire the two for going eleven minutes and fifteen seconds with the bear.

Whispers of an affair between June Byers and Billy Wolfe got a boost when Wolfe joined Byers in Louisville that weekend to attend the Derby and make a play at ownership of a Derby horse. Wolfe was spotted with Byers in a downtown hotel lobby the morning of the race waiting for Walter Fugate, owner of Derby participant Hallieboy. Wolfe had his eye on buying an interest in the horse and hoped to close the deal prior to the race.

Fugate joined Wolfe and Byers, who was dressed to the nines and looked completely bored by the horse talk. The two men hammered out a verbal agreement, settling on a $15,000 price for half ownership of the colt. Fugate asked Wolfe to meet him at stall fifteen in the Churchill Downs paddocks a few hours later to finalize the deal. The publicity hound Wolfe told Fugate to invite the press to capture the moment.

Wolfe and Fugate met as planned, but by the time Wolfe arrived, he had soured him on the deal and backed out. *The Washington Post* claimed Wolfe had been talked out of the deal by his attorney. News that Hallieboy collapsed upon arrival at Churchill Downs after a 37 hour drive from Lincoln Downs in Rhode Island probably doomed the deal.

Per *The Richmond News Leader*, which also reported Ginger the Wrestling Bear's appearance in the Derby city, "Hallieboy is a corn pone entry from Georgia, out to prove that not only the caviar-rich can own a Derby horse." The garland of roses went to Middleground, who went on to win the Belmont Stakes and place second in the Preakness. Hallieboy, a 100 to 1 shot, came in tenth in a field of fourteen.

According to *The Washington Post*, both June Byers and Mildred Burke accompanied Billy Wolfe to stall fifteen to call off the deal for Hallieboy. Burke wrestled Mae Weston Des Moines on May 3 and Waterloo, Iowa on May 7. It's possible Burke traveled to Louisville in between contests to attend the Derby with her estranged husband. It's also likely, given her close resemblance to the champ, the *Post* reporter had mistaken a dolled up Mars Bennett for the champ.

ALL PRETTY FOR TV

A story put out on the United Press wire right after the Kentucky Derby by Oscar Fraley painted a portrait of domestic bliss between Billy Wolfe and Mildred Burke, who could "toss off a steak or a rival wrestler with equal aplomb." Wolfe was certainly at the height of his power. He told Fraley the diamonds he wore in public totaled thirty grand in value, and women continued to flock to Al Haft's Gym in Columbus for a shot at fortune and glory. Mildred Burke's biographer Jeff Leen noted that Billy Wolfe had created a life for himself only rivaled by Hollywood moguls of the day and Hugh Hefner a few years later. He had a successful business empire, and he was constantly surrounded by beautiful women.

But at the time Fraley's story hit the wire, the relationship between Burke and Wolfe had never been more strained. Burke could sense her "husband" was looking for someone to replace her, and not just in the home. Just as Vince McMahon would later declare, "I created Hulkamania, and I'm gonna kill it!" Billy Wolfe believed he had created Milliemania. He could tear her down at will and replace her whenever he liked.

And he had just the girl in mind: Nell Stewart.

Just as June Byers had come into her own, so too had "Pretty" Nell Stewart. The Alabama Assassin had a rags-to-riches story to rival that of Burke and Byers. After losing her father at the age of fourteen, she became the primary breadwinner for the family, waiting tables and saving up tips to support her mother and brothers.

Mae Young spotted the athletic girl in the diner in 1943 when she was just fifteen. She had her first match at age sixteen in Mexico and was mentored on the road by Gladys Gillem, who grew to hate the girl when she supplanted Gillem as Billy Wolfe's mistress.

Wolfe controlled Stewart's diet and exercise regimen. He had her hair dyed blonde and remade the girl in the image of the most popular movie star of the time, Betty Grable. By 1950 she was averaging $25,000 a year. And yes, she had her own collection of diamonds.

Wolfe kept June and Nell apart just as he isolated all of the ladies from Mildred, for obvious reasons. While June had three inches and ten pounds of muscle on Nell, the blonde beauty was the clear front runner to become the next champion.

Burke knew this better than anyone. She despised Stewart. She considered the girl from Alabama to be a terrible wrestler, unfit even for consideration as champion. She made it clear she would never do the honors for Billy's bleach blonde beauty.

If Nell was to be the next champion, though, what would become of June Byers? On paper, the Texas Tornado seemed a much better choice than the Alabama Assassin. She had three inches height on Nell Stewart and five inches on the champ. She didn't have the movie star body Nell Stewart did, but this was pro wrestling, not the movies.

Some fans loved June. Some hated her. It didn't matter at the box office. They all bought tickets when she came to town.

June appeared in wire story by Ed O'Neill printed in the New York *Daily News* on July 16, 1950. "Once confined to burlesque houses, carnivals, and circus peep shows, girl wrestling is today a $2,000,000 business that attracts thousands of fans in 42 states — New York not included — and pays off handsomely to a growing number of gals flexing their biceps in rings all over the country."

O'Neill, who was pictured in some papers being stretched and twisted by Millie Stafford and Mars Bennett, sang the praises of Millie Stafford, Bennett, and Byers in particular. Through 900 bouts, said O'Neill, June had earned thousands of dollars, a collection of eye-catching diamonds, a limousine with custom red upholstery, and a collection of more than fifty injuries, including broken collarbones (both left and right), a fractured back, torn cartilage in both knees, injuries to every one of her ten fingers, and multiple black eyes.

Unfortunately, *Daily News* readers would have to travel to New Jersey to see the action live, as the New York Athletic Commission of the time refused to give sanction to women's wrestling. Or, they could simply take advantage of the latest technology taking the country by storm. "There being no law against television...the girls cross the state line via televised matches."

Television started out as a controversial subject in the wrestling business. While some promoters were seeing dollar signs, many wrestlers feared that live broadcasts would cut into the live gates and thus, their pay. A group of men even staged a temporary strike in California over the issue.

Fears that television would kill live wrestling ultimately proved to be unfounded. The live broadcast was the best possible advertising for a sport that was ready-made for the small screen. Television introduced pro wrestling to new fans, and TV-ready star Gorgeous George was sometimes credited with selling as many TV sets as Milton Berle.

June Byers proved to be one of the breakout stars on TV. As early as 1949, promoters were clamoring for June to appear on their broadcast. And yes, that included the New York fans whose only opportunity to see women's wrestling was on television.

June's smile appeared alongside Dennis Day, Judy Canova, Fred Waring, and others in a summer newspaper ad for WLW-T Channel 4 in Cincinnati, promoting a live match with Lilly Bitter. Bitter was one of the newest girls on the road, an eighteen-year-old who, a few years earlier, had organized a fan club for her favorite grappler Tony Galento. Standing 5'5" with an official weight of 135 pounds, Bitter wrestled barefoot, saying that socks and boots slowed her down too much in the ring.

June spoke about the challenges of wrestling on television to Jim Melby in 1984. "T.V. certainly changed the nature of the sport. You had to learn to become a more dynamic performer as you had a smaller medium and time element to work with. Change is the only constant thing in life. Before me men like Joe Stecher and Strangler Lewis would wrestle matches that would go on for hours. They concentrated on pitting strength against strength. The same is true today, but techniques have changed, wrestling has become faster and faster."

On July 31, June appeared in the Cincinnati papers again. She was back to wrestle on WLW-T, this time for the women's world championship. Even though Mildred Burke was the world champion, it was June, smiling and in a full body shot, featured in the ad.

"Do not be surprised if Miss Byers beats Miss Burke and takes the title," promoter Joe Gunther told the *Birmingham Post-Herald*. "Everywhere Miss Byers is regarded as the number one title contender, and many think she is Miss Burke's superior. She certainly has looked great in local starts."

Gunther's ballyhoo takes on added meaning when you know his back story. The Alabama promoter got his start working for Chris Jordan. More than a decade before Gunther promoted Burke vs. Byers, Chris Jordan hyped a match between Women's World Champion Clara Mortensen and the young, hungry challenger Mildred Burke.

Miss Byers did not take Miss Burke's title that summer. It was June's job, once again, to put the champ over. Burke and Byers drew crowds in Tennessee, Louisiana, Alabama, and Florida, where they set a new attendance record in Panama City.

It was during this time that the numbers the ladies drew in Boston swelled unexpectedly. While the papers reported 10,000 in 1948 and 5,000 in 1949, promoters were throwing a much larger figure, claiming Burke and Byers had drawn 15,000 in the city.

This wasn't uncommon in professional wrestling, and in the case of women's wrestling it wasn't even close to the largest such exaggeration. It was long believed Mildred Burke and Elvira Snodgrass drew the largest crowd ever for a women's show in Louisville, Kentucky with a reported number of 18,000 paying over $25,000. The actual attendance for the show in the Jefferson County Armory was just over 7100, near capacity for the building at the time, with a gate of $4350.

A Hazard, Kentucky gal named Cora Combs had her first taste of action against June Byers in the fall of 1950. Combs was a country music singer before she gave pro wrestling a go. After a crash course in Columbus with the boss, she found herself in the ring with the veteran the new girls feared most.

Yet while many lady grapplers found it difficult to say nice things about Byers later in life, Combs was one of the exceptions. "June Byers, she's the one that took charge of me. She was lovely. She was strict on me, you know, and everything like that. She was a good person."

Byers and Combs spent a lot of time on the road together, traveling to Ohio, Pennsylvania, and up and down the East Coast through November of 1950. Combs said that of all the veterans, Byers helped her the most. She also said that Byers was very well respected. "Yes she was. She demanded it."

Byers finished the year feuding with another rookie who becoming a close friend, Mars Bennett. Older and more mature than most lady wrestlers, Bennett was never afraid to march to the beat her own drum. When Billy Wolfe and Mildred Burke's marriage imploded a few years later, Bennett would jump ship briefly and work for promoter Jack Pfefer. By the mid-fifties, after nearly marrying a New York jeweler and future *F-Troop* star Larry Storch, Bennett was in a not-so-secret relationship with fellow lady wrestler Belle Drummond.

Bennett was an ideal opponent for Byers. Having taken bumps off horses, elephants, and circus apparatus for years, she could take the licks Byers dished out and deliver a few hard knocks of her own, always with her own million dollar smile. Byers gave Mars a cut over her left eye one night that required four stitches. That didn't stop them from enjoying down time together with Billy Boy and June's dogs in tow.

TURNING POINTS

"Wrestling isn't easy, never has been. You've got to apply yourself mentally and physically. You must be able to take the bows as well as the boos."

June Byers spoke with The *M'Alester News-Capital* in McAlester, Oklahoma prior to her match there with Mars Bennett in December of 1950, sharing some of her backstory and reflecting on how far she'd come. While the emphasis was on her upcoming bout with Mars Bennett, the subject inevitably turned to Mildred Burke.

"She learned the hard way too, but look where Mildred is today — a champion, well respected, and a very healthy, wealthy woman. Now there is a lady."

If June didn't truly respect Mildred Burke, she put on a good front. As 1951 began, her job depended on it. June traveled to Oklahoma for a New Year's Day appointment with Burke in Tulsa. June won the first fall, but Burke came back to take the second and third in front of 3500 fans. For the next two weeks, they packed houses in Texas, Oklahoma, Arkansas, Missouri, and even Memphis, Tennessee.

Wrestling and TV Sports magazine ran a story on June in January of 1951. June recounted the story of learning to wrestle from her "Uncle" Ottoway while reiterating her desire to become a promoter after her wrestling days were over.

"The only way you can learn to be a promoter is to be actively engaged in the sport. I have wrestled in every state in the union and in several foreign countries. Do you realize that there are only two women promoters in the country, neither of whom were competitors such as I? One is Mrs. Max Yeargain of Topeka, Kansas, who took over the reins after her husband died; the other is Mrs. Florence Turner of

Washington, DC. Both have used the feminine approach and it has paid off handsomely."

The three-page story on the "girl of the future" featured photos of June in the ring as well as images of the lady away from the ring. One image showed June demonstrating a hold on a male friend. Another showed her feeding her roommate's toddler, and third featured June enjoying a game of bowling. In addition to the requisite bowling shoes, she was in full makeup, her curly hair perfectly set, wearing a skirt with a lacy top.

June returned to Ohio mid-month to work with Gloria Barattini, a 5'6" native of Laurel, Maryland who also happened to be a classically trained opera singer. Barattini was cast as the babyface in Cincinnati for a star-studded live broadcast benefiting the Polio Fund. More than 3000 fans turned up at the Music Hall that night, and between the live crowd and operators taking calls from viewers, the show raised $15,000.

Charity or no charity, June chose not to pull any punches that night. In fact she manhandled the referee in a losing effort, an attack that drew the ire of the Cincinnati Boxing and Wrestling Commission. State and local athletic commissions were generally staffed by political cronies, many of whom were fans but knew very little of how promoters conducted business, especially when it came to wrestling.

Byers wasn't the only one causing trouble. Joe Christie and Kala Kwaraini also angered the Commission by continuing to fight after their bouts had ended. All three wrestlers were suspended, banned from wrestling in Cincinnati for the next six months. What's more, the commission ordered wrestling promoter Ross Leader to attend their next meeting where the Commission would consider banning women's wrestling entirely.

Cincinnati Post sports editor Pat Harmon was on hand when the Commission had it out with Ross Leader in early February. Part of the discussion centered on the pay for the referees and wrestlers on the charity show. The commission was outraged Leader had shorted the refs, paying $40 instead of the requisite $75. Leader said he'd spoken to two members of the commission about the $40 pay day and been given a verbal okay since it was a charity show. Both of the members named denied giving their consent, and the commission voted to charge Leader for the amount shorted.

The Commission asked Leader if he'd bartered with the wrestlers to get them to take less than their standard fees, since the event was for charity. Leader told them it was none of their business.

As for women's wrestling, it certainly seemed likely a permanent ban might happen, but Commission members were reminded there were two types of lady wrestlers: the unladylike, including June Byers, and the well-mannered. The consensus was that it would be unfair to the latter group to punish them for the actions of the former, Miss Byers in particular. Byers' suspension remained in effect, but women's wrestling in Cincinnati was saved.

"If the fights in the ring are as stimulating as those at headquarters," Pat Harmon wrote, "Cincinnati fans are in for a great year."

June was far from the Queen City when the Cincinnati authorities ruled on women's wrestling. After traveling to Florida to wrestle Violet Viann for a few days, by the end of the month she was in Louisville to kick off another round of matches with the champion. For most of February and March she bounced up and down the East Coast, working mostly with Lilly Bitter and Cincinnati-born Sheba Zenni. Billed as an Assyrian Princess, Zenni was the youngest of twelve children in a Lebanese family, a strikingly beautiful woman who only wrestled for a brief time.

Burke notched a few more victories over Byers in Ohio before June went back on the road with Gloria Barattini. Barattini and Zenni got the worst of it from June that spring, with Barattini suffering two broken ribs the night June tossed her out of the ring in Charlotte. Occasionally one or the other would score a win from the Texas Tornado, but only by mercy. The refs would have enough of June's roughhouse actions and disqualify her.

You have to think her one-on-one sessions with June Byers may have been a reason why Sheba Zinni didn't stick around!

In late May, Byers and Burke locked up in Texas, wrestling on May 22 in Fort Worth, May 23 in San Antonio, and May 24 in Corpus Christi, where the finish came in an unexpected manner. After splitting the first two falls, as they had often done before, June lost the third not by pin but disqualification after tossing Mildred Burke over the top rope.

Several more title matches were scheduled for early June, but Ann Laverne, who wrestled a handful of matches with June to end the month of May, was sent in as a replacement.

It's unclear what caused June's sudden cancellation, but she would be out of action for the remainder of the year. *The State* in Columbia, South Carolina said June suffered a sudden attack of appendicitis. The *News and Record* in Greensboro said June canceled because of "ill health." The Louisville *Courier-Journal* stated on June 24 that Byers was home recovering from two operations.

Whatever the cause, the time off gave June Byers some well-deserved rest.

June was on the sidelines when one of the greatest tragedies of the era took place. While wrestling the first of two matches in East Liverpool on July 27, 1951, a rookie named Janet Boyer Wolfe took a hard body slam from Ella Waldek, a twenty-one-year-old former roller derby girl from Washington state. The match continued, with Waldek getting a win in only seven minutes, and the ladies retired to the locker room.

Janet Wolfe began complaining of a headache some time later. Waldek said she urged the girl to tell Billy Wolfe she was feeling ill, but Janet refused. She had to return to the ring to tag up with Eva Lee against Waldek and Mae Young.

Wolfe began the match with Mae Young, working just a few moments before signaling to Lee she wanted to tag out. Lee stepped into the ring. Wolfe stepped out onto the apron. Lee, Waldek, Young, and the crowd gasped as Wolfe collapsed.

The match was stopped immediately. A doctor in attendance tended to the girl in the building before she was rushed to the hospital. She would never regain consciousness. Born on June 13, 1931, Wolfe was eighteen and barely a month when she died.

Waldek, Lee, and Young were held for questioning but released. It took a few days for the autopsy results to determine Wolfe died of a brain hemorrhage caused by a blood clot that had formed several days before the show in East Liverpool. The evidence clearly proved Waldek was not at fault, but chants of "Murderer!" would haunt her for the rest of her career.

No one took the death of Janet Wolfe harder than Billy Wolfe. He first met Janet when she was only sixteen years old, and he had become her legal guardian so that he could take her under his wing and training the then underage girl. Janet's birth mother never blamed Wolfe. She believed it was an accident and could have happened to anyone.

With the death of Janet Boyer Wolfe, the inevitable fall Billy Wolfe's women's wrestling empire had begun. Fans and the press resumed the debate over whether women's wrestling should be allowed. Some cities and athletic commissions considered bans.

Business would take another hit that fall, when Mildred Burke and Billy Wolfe's son G. Bill were in a car accident. G. Bill would spend months in a full body cast. Burke suffered multiple injuries, including five broken ribs that would keep her out of the ring until the start of 1952. Billy Wolfe now had two of his biggest draws, his wife and June Byers, on the sidelines.

The accident also sped up the unraveling of the long-standing affair between Mildred Burke and Billy Wolfe's son. Shortly before the accident, G. Bill had approached his father with a shocking demand. He wanted Billy to divorce Mildred so that he could marry her.

Billy laid down the law with his son. G. Bill could marry any lady wrestler he wanted, except Nell Stewart. Or, he could carry on his relationship with Mildred Burke. But under no circumstances would the father divorce his wife so his son could marry her.

G. Bill's long convalescence, coupled with a growing drinking problem, would ultimately lead to the end of the affair with Mildred Burke. The son would side with the father, and when he did marry, the news would be a crushing blow to his ex-lover.

STRIKING GOLD

No one hoped for better fortunes at the dawn of 1952 than Billy Wolfe. The tragedy of Janet Wolfe was behind him. His two big stars, Mildred Burke and June Byers, were ready to get back on the road. His marriage was clearly headed for an end, but his son was back in the fold, and the promoter was ready to replace Mildred Burke with Nell Stewart.

One question still remained: what would he do with June Byers? Now seven years into the business, she was as worthy of championship gold as any woman. When she returned to action in February, the press hailed her as Number Three, with only Nell Stewart and Mildred Burke ranked ahead of her.

Beverly Lehmer was June's first victim upon her return. The Iowa girl had become a pro wrestler by accident. Her sister Carolyn was a fan and wanted to join the ranks of lady wrestlers, but in order to train, Carolyn needed a training partner. The reluctant sister proved to be a good hand in the ring, which is how she ended up in the ring with a rested and riled up June Byers in Tennessee.

"When she hit you, you knew you were hit," said Beverly Lehmer. "I didn't like wrestling her. She'd give you those hits, and she'd hurt you."

June Byers also got her hands on Ella Waldek in March. As tough as Waldek was, she hated working with June. Byers probably had a little more sting in her strikes than normal, and who can blame her? She was back in action, back to making money and living a life that had been exceedingly good to her and her son.

And she, like everyone else, could smell blood in the water as the Wolfe-Burke relationship disintegrated.

June received a warmer welcome when she set foot in the ring with the equally rough and rugged Elvira Snodgrass. One of the few women still remaining from the late 1930s, Elvira had once been the Number Two woman herself. She'd settled into a veteran's role, playing the heel and getting the new girls over while making sure each one paid their dues.

Sadly, Elvira's time in the ring would come to an end in June, 1952. Of all the tales told about Cousin Elvira, none speak to her toughness and resilience more than the accident story. While driving home from a show late one night in the month of June, Elvira's car rolled into a ditch just outside Florence, Kentucky. She had the driver's window down, and her arm was outside the vehicle when the accident happened. Her arm was pinned between the dirt and the car, so... she cut off her own arm to escape the wreck and flag down help.

Newspaper accounts of the time record that her arm was injured and later amputated in the hospital, but her surviving family members, including the niece who was living with her when she died of cardiac arrest a few years later, swear by the tale. Some even claim that Elvira came back and wrestled a time or two after with only one arm.

When Penny Banner hit the road with Mae Young a few years later, she was taken to meet "the greatest of all girl wrestlers." Mae drove Penny to the Columbus, Ohio home Elvira shared with her third husband. Mae made the introductions and then instructed the rookie to bow down and call her "Majesty."

One of June's final matches with Elvira put the two veterans on one side of the ring opposite Ella Waldek and Millie Stafford on March 29. There's no recap in the Sikeston, Missouri newspaper, so we're left to speculate just how black and blue Stafford and Waldek looked when they left the arena that night.

That being said, June must have seen something in Millie Stafford she liked. Stafford was still fairly new to the wrestling game. The two had first worked together prior to June's eight month hiatus, wrestling on live TV in Cincinnati. Stafford was from Minnesota and had worked as a telephone operator before training with Einar Olsen.

In order to set her apart and give her some "flavor," she was often promoted as being French.

June tagged with several younger wrestlers in the first half of 1952, including Ella Waldek and Ruth Boatcallie, a fellow Texan who had been trained by Elvira Snodgrass. By July, however, she settled into a regular partnership with Stafford, and together, the ladies would become champions.

The team of Byers and Stafford won their first tag match at Turner's Arena in Washington, D.C. on July 9. The following night in Wilmington, Delaware, they defeated the team of Carol Cook and Lilly Bitter for the second night in a row. The same four ladies wrestled in Staunton, Virginia on the 14th and a rematch in Wilmington on the 17th. Wilmington's regular referee Bob Wade, who had a devil of a time during the July 10 bout, was relieved to sit back and watch when Ruth Boatcallie officiated the rematch.

Byers and Stafford took a break from tagging up in August, working separately in singles. Byers worked a few tags with other partners near the end of the month, including Terry Majors and Betty Jo Hawkins. They came back together in September, this time with a trophy the duo had won "some time ago" that designated them as the Women's Tag Team Champions.

The first mention of the titles appears in the *El Paso Times*, where the local promoter hyped a singles match between Millie Stafford and Lilly Bitter. Bitter is portrayed as one of the top five women while Stafford was said to have recently become a champion with Byers. Byers was in Louisville that same day, wrestling Terry Majors and Lois Johnson with tag partner Betty Jo Hawkins.

The *Republican and Herald* of Pottsville, Pennsylvania was next to name Byers and Stafford as tag champs on September 4. On that date, the *Ridgewood Herald-News* in New Jersey promoted a contest in which Millie Stafford and Lilly Bitters would wrestle June Byers and Carol Carota.

On September 10, *The Jersey Journal* of Jersey announced a championship bout pitting Byers and Stafford against Carol Carota and

Lilly Bitter. Stafford and Byers were named as champions, but the promotional ad stated that a $1000 trophy would be awarded to the winners "for the first time." *The Bayonne Times* followed suit the next day announcing the use of a $1000 trophy to crown the tag team champs that very evening.

So when, and where, and how exactly did Byers and Stafford become champions? Enter George Sherman, sports reporter for the *St. Joseph Gazette* in St. Joseph, Missouri, who presented the following improbable explanation on the same day of the announcement in *The Bayonne Times*.

"Millie Stafford and June Byers recently won the women's world tag team wrestling championship and were presented with a gigantic trophy by Ned Brown, executive editor of the *NWA Official Wrestling Magazine*. The trophy, one of the biggest ever given in professional wrestling, was awarded in Texas following a series of elimination matches which lasted more than three months with 64 fem teams participating. It marked the first time the National Wrestling Alliance has given official recognition to a women's title aside from Mildred Burke's world championship."

As epic as a 64 team tournament would have been, it's doubtful there were 128 active women's wrestlers in 1952. The fans had no way to fact check the story, so it stuck. It wouldn't be the last time a women's championship tournament was fabricated out of thin air.

June did plenty of wrestling in Texas in the months leading up to George Sherman's proclamation, but none of those matches were tag contests. But hey, this was 1952. There was no Internet. There was no cable TV. And magazines like the *NWA Official Wrestling Magazine* carefully constructed the reality the promoters wanted to present.

Millie Stafford and June Byers were women's world tag team champions and had a $1000 trophy to prove it. So there.

June and Millie worked more singles matches than tags, but over the coming months, the girls defended their $1000 trophy against teams like Ida Mae Martinez and Lilly Bitter, Ella Waldek and Carol Carota, Ella Waldek and Ethel Brown, Ella Waldek and Dot Dotson,

Dolores Villa and Ethel Brown, and Ida Mae Martinez and Bonnie Watson.

"I will never forget a tag team match in Mexico City against Ella Waldek and Mae Young," Byers told Jim Melby in 1984. "I did well in tag team matches."

The duo of Stafford and Byers were never defeated for their $1000 trophy, but some time after their November 21 victory over Waldek and Brown, Stafford and Byers called it quits. Shortly after Christmas, June was in Tucson, Arizona, where her new protege Mary Jane Mull filled in for the "injured" Millie Stafford in a match with Ida Mae Martinez and Betty Alexander. By January 5, the team of Mary Jane Mull and June Byers had become the new women's tag team champions.

The early explanation for the split between Byers and Stafford was that Stafford had been injured and needed to take time off to heal. Stafford worked a light schedule in December and January, but she did not take any significant time off. Byers would later claim that Stafford had chosen to retire, but Millie Stafford continued wrestling a full schedule throughout the 1950s with her final match coming in 1971.

A few weeks after the Byers-Mull team became official *The Lincoln Star* in Nebraska offered this tidbit: "When Miss Stafford arrived at the point that she didn't trust June's judgment, Miss Byers promptly ditched her in favor of Mary Jane Mull, her former protege and one who follows her strategy without question."

The logic is sound: the veteran, portrayed by *The Lincoln Star* as the team leader, chose a younger wrestler willing to listen over a girl who didn't see eye to eye with her. But Millie Stafford's January schedule offers another clue as to why Byers and Stafford didn't see eye to eye. While Byers and Mull were defending their tag team trophy, Millie Stafford was wrestling Mildred Burke for the Women's World Championship.

The marriage between Mildred Burke and Billy Wolfe had finally come to an end by this time. With the matrimonial divorce now official, the much messier business divorce was just kicking off. Burke intended to take the business over from Wolfe, and many of the ladies were following her. June Byers stayed with Billy Wolfe, and if Millie Stafford did indeed follow Mildred Burke out the door, that certainly would have put an end to her partnership with Byers.

After just a couple of matches as the fill-in, Mull was declared to be co-champion with Byers. The official story was that Mull had won a tournament to select a new partner for Byers after Stafford was injured. Mull worked a series of battle royals with June before and after New Year's, but just like the phantom Texas tag tournament of the summer of 1952, there was no tournament to choose a new partner for June.

Mull was said to be a native of Cincinnati who took a job as a department store model in Toledo after graduating high school. Mull took an interest in professional wrestling after seeing Nell Stewart in action and decided a chance of career was in order. Standing 5′5″ and weighing 138 pounds, she made a powerful ally in the ring for the 5′7″ Byers.

THE SECRETARY

A woman who made the journey to Columbus, Ohio to try her luck at Al Haft's Gym, had a dream. She wanted to be famous. She wanted to see her name in lights. She wanted people to stare at the diamonds and furs dripping off her as she traveled from one town to the next.

She did not want to sit at a desk and take dictation. She did not want to be associated with a job title like "Secretary."

In early 1953 newspapers across the country announced that Nell Stewart had, in fact, become a secretary. Far from a receptionist that took dictation, hers was an honorary title, more so than most who became "secretary" of a newly founded company.

Nell was one of the officers for Girl Wrestling Enterprises, an organization created to promote women's wrestling all across the country. Nell Stewart, the number two girl in the business, was named the organization's secretary, and June Byers, number three, was designated as the company's treasurer.

Not that the founding father had any intention of letting June even think about touching the money! Girl Wrestling Enterprises was, after all, the brainchild of Billy Wolfe in partnership with his prodigal son, G. Bill. Fresh off his divorce from Mildred Burke, having just sold Mildred his half of the company he co-owned with her, Attractions, Inc., Billy Wolfe created Girl Wrestling Enterprises so he could once again promote the sport of women's wrestling.

It didn't matter a whit to Billy Wolfe that he'd signed an agreement saying that he could never promote women's wrestling again. Wolfe never had any intention of getting out of the lucrative enterprise he co-founded. He gave Burke her divorce. He allowed her to buy him out of Attractions, Inc., a deal that put her $30,000 in debt.

He gave her a piece of paper with his signature on it that said he'd never, ever try to compete with her. The he filed papers with the State of Ohio to start a new company that would compete directly with his ex-wife.

If Mildred Burke believed she would get support from the National Wrestling Alliance, the organization that negotiated the sale of Billy Wolfe's half of Attractions, Inc. to Burke, she was sadly mistaken. The NWA wanted little to do with women's wrestling and nothing to do with women promoters. The few allies she had in the business could only sit back and watch. Even Lou Thesz, the great Heavyweight Champion who had no love for the sport of women's wrestling, took pity on Burke, warning her to watch her back.

Naming Stewart and Byers as officers of the new company was a stroke of genius. It gave Wolfe just enough legal cover to claim he had not broken his agreement. Writing in Omaha's *The Evening World-Herald* on March 25, 1953, columnist Floyd Olds explained that it was Burke's rivals Nell Stewart and June Byers who had split from her to form Girl Wrestling Enterprises.

"Billy Wolfe, who has been the tycoon of women's rassling for more than 20 years, has abdicated, and his former grapplers have split up into two groups."

Olds explained that while Burke would retain control of Attractions, Inc., "Nell Stewart heads the cast for a rival organization known as Girl Wrestling Enterprises. She is joined by June Byers, Mary Jane Mull, Violet Viann, Ida Mae Martinez, and a number of other girls who were shown the way to mat riches by Billy Wolfe."

The NWA welcomed Girl Wrestling Enterprises with open arms, comparing the new business rivalry in girl wrestling to the competition half a century earlier between the American and National Leagues in baseball. Behind the scenes, the majority of NWA members had no desire to see Mildred Burke succeed. Her request to become a member the NWA was denied. While never stated publicly, the NWA was strictly a "boys" club, and they'd already taken sides.

The ladies began choosing up sides. Knowing Wolfe had

always taken fifty percent of his wrestlers' earnings, Burke dropped her commission to forty percent. Girl Wrestling Enterprises dropped theirs to twenty-five percent.

Oddly enough, the women's wrestling business was not the only part of the industry seeing fractions in its ranks. On April 17, 1953, the *Transcript-Telegram* of Holyoke, Massachusetts reported that the midgets were also splitting into two different organizations. Emerging out of the Montreal territory in the late 1940s, midget wrestling became hugely popular thanks to the efforts of promoter Jack Britton. But success breeds competition, and just as Moolah would supplant Billy Wolfe in women's wrestling, Lord Littlebrook would succeed Britton as the go-to booker for midget wrestlers.

Burke's bid to run her own women's booking office might have had a better chance of succeeding if the business in general was not experiencing a downturn. The TV bubble had burst. Women's wrestling, after nearly a decade of immense popularity, was no longer the attraction it had once been. And Girl Wrestling Enterprises was not the only force pushing a new champion. Clara Mortensen, who had lost the championship to Burke in 1938, staked her claim based on a little-publicized match Burke lost to Mortensen years before in Chattanooga, Tennessee. Lillian Ellison, now known as Slave Girl Moolah, also laid claim to being the Women's Champion.

Girl Wrestling Enterprises and Baltimore promoter Ed Contos announced that a tournament would be held on April 14, 1953 to officially crown a new Women's World Champion. While the press releases made the tournament sound like an open invitation affair, Burke never received one. Nor did Billy Wolfe send one. Wolfe had tried for years to get Mildred Burke to drop the belt to Nell Stewart. She wouldn't do it, and not even a savage beating from her husband would persuade her to change her mind. What's more, Nell didn't have the skills to take the belt by force. With the announcement of a new women's title, it seemed as if Nell's day was finally about to arrive.

June Byers was among those announced for the tournament, and she kept a busy schedule in the days leading up to Baltimore. After wrestling Lilly Bitters on television on Cincinnati on the 4th, she worked a double shot in Sandusky, Ohio on the 6th, losing a singles match to Lilly Bitter via disqualification and a tag match with Mary Jane Mull to Bitter and Ida Mae Martinez, also by disqualification.

June and Lilly locked up again on the evening of April 8, each scoring one fall a piece before the match was declared a no-contest. The match capped off an eventful day for June Byers. Earlier that same day, in Franklin, Ohio, June married Billy Wolfe's son, G. Bill.

G. Bill was just a few months older than his new bride, born February 22, 1922. It's hard to say if there was any real love between the couple or if this was a marriage arranged to keep business in the family. Squeezing a wedding into a busy road schedule on route to a major tournament certainly speaks to the latter.

The news of G. Bill's marriage to June Byers added insult to injury for Burke. It's no wonder she decided to throw a pipe bomb into Baltimore six days later.

A NEW CHAMPION

"Congratulations to Ed Contos for promoting a tournament in which Nell Stewart is to win from nobody. I wrestled Nell Stewart last year in seven matches for the title and defeated her seven straight falls. These were the last matches she wrestled me.

"No champion in history has ever defended his title that many times in succession against one opponent. This wire is dated and timed before the Baltimore tournament. Donna Marie Dieckman tried to enter the tournament but was denied."

One can only imagine the rage and anger Ed Contos and Billy Wolfe felt upon reading those words. They were sent via telegram to the sports editor at the *Baltimore Sun* by Mildred Burke herself, who saw the Baltimore tournament for what it was: an attempt to usurp her as the Women's World Champion.

Nell Stewart was certainly the fan favorite. She'd been pushed to the moon, made to look like a champion for years by Wolfe. What was obvious to the fans was very apparent to every woman who made the trek to Baltimore. This was Nell's night. Her big pay-off. Her reward for giving Billy Wolfe what he wanted while being the good soldier and putting Burke over for so long.

The men in the smoke-filled room debated their options. They could still go through with the plan and put the new women's championship belt on Nell Stewart. This wasn't the first time someone had tried to subvert a wrestling show by indirectly revealing insider baseball. Jack Pfefer had been doing such nonsense for years. Public opinion and box office receipts had taken hits because of his actions, but the fans had always come back.

Nell winning would be a message to Mildred Burke. No doubt Billy wanted to stick to the plan for that very reason. He'd be out of

Baltimore the day after, on to the next city. But Ed Contos would have another show to produce. The Maryland State Athletic Commission would feel the pinch as well. And who knows if Burke was done sending poison-pen telegrams.

Billy Wolfe was prepared for the moment. He had another champion in waiting. Her time would come now, rather than later.

And Nell?

Love her or hate her, you have to feel for Nell.

Ed Contos, Sr., promoted shows on Tuesday nights in Baltimore for nearly a quarter of a century. The colorful promoter was known as much for his own war of words with Chief Magistrate Stanley Scherr as the grunt-and-groan action he gave the people of Baltimore. In 1937, when Scherr discovered wrestlers were using fake blood in some of their matches, he proclaimed that Athletic Association of Maryland would henceforth refer to wrestling as an exhibition. Contos replied simply, "Wrestling is more honest than fishing."

A member of the NWA and a close friend of Columbus promoter Al Haft, Ed Contos made a great case for staging the women's tournament. While the NWA had unified promotions around a men's World Champion, the organization had never formally recognized a women's title. Mildred Burke's championship had its roots in Al Haft's Midwest Wrestling Association, not the NWA, and in the mid-1950s she was one of a handful of women laying claim to being the world champion.

"Miss Lillian Ellison is claiming because her manager so decrees," Contos told the press. "Miss Clara Mortenson is the titleholder according to her father, and Miss Mildred Burke has been another claimant for a number of years."

While Contos had the blessing of NWA President Sam Muchnick to proceed, the entire affair smelled of collusion. The facts put out in the media were all truthful. The tournament had the sanction of the Maryland State Athletic Commission as well as the NWA and Billy Wolfe, the man responsible for booking most of the lady wrestlers.

But a few key facts were omitted from the record. Wolfe was no longer booking Mildred Burke, and while the stated purpose of the event was to bring clarity to a crowded women's title picture, no one invited Lillian Ellison, Clara Mortensen, or Mildred Burke.

Every woman in the locker room that night in Baltimore received her marching orders from Billy Wolfe: Nell, June, Lilly Bitter, Gloria Shelton, Violet Viann, Joyce Ford, Ida Mae Martinez, and Mary Jane Mull.

June Byers kicked off the night with a 22 minute match against Lilly Bitter. After Byers pinned Bitter, Nell Stewart went into action, defeating Gloria Shelton in only nine minutes. Violet Viann defeated Joyce Ford in ten minutes. Ida Mae Martinez pinned Mary Jane Mull in fourteen minutes to end the first round of action.

The semi-finals kicked off with June Byers ending Violet Viann's night in a 14 minute bout. Nell Stewart defeated Ida Mae Martinez in twelve minutes, setting the stage for the final.

What could have been a slam-bang climax ended with a whimper. It only took five minutes for June Byers to pin Nell Stewart, the heavy favorite, to become the Women's World Champion. Jim Holmes, chairman of the Maryland State Athletic Commission, handed the newly-minted women's championship belt to Byers.

"The crowd saw only five minutes of wrestling, but they long will remember those five minutes!" So goes the write up in the NWA magazine that reeks of the Billy Wolfe spin machine. "June, fresh as if this was the first match of the evening, went after her opponent from the tap of the bell and didn't let up for a second. In just five minutes she had Nell Stewart pinned with an arm lock and body press in as neat a fall as anyone would wish to see. For a moment the vast crowd was stunned but realizing what happened they gave the new champion the biggest ovation a woman wrestler ever received in any ring."

The finish may well have taken the air out of the building. The fans had been primed for a Nell Stewart victory, but the five-minute finale was the shortest match of the night. Mildred Burke's biographer Jeff Leen offers a gut-wrenching assessment of the strangely short affair in *Queen of the Ring*. "Stewart no doubt had no stomach to put on a lengthy, worked match with Byers and had opted to limit the torture by getting things over as quickly as possible."

Penny Banner might have come closest to getting Nell Stewart's side of the tale. In her autobiography *Banner Days*, Penny recounts a conversation the two had shortly after becoming tag partners.

Impressed by the newbie's ring work, Nell asked Penny how she'd learned to wrestle. When Penny gave credit to Byers for mopping the floor with her night after night, Nell laughed. "Byers is one tough cookie."

Banner says Nell then told her that Byers had "robbed her" of the championship match she should have had against Mildred Burke in 1954.

"What happened?" Banner asked.

"It's a long story." Nell never said another word about it.

"I knew Byers was a true champion," Banner wrote. "She always beat them square in the middle of the ring, so it couldn't have been that. Nell never said any more, and I never asked. But I always wondered."

Byers herself never harbored any ill feelings toward Nell Stewart. At least, that's what she said in a 1993 interview. "I always thought Nell was a great wrestler. If anyone knows if [she's] still alive or how to contact [her], please let me know." If Nell's feelings were different, you can hardly blame her.

Two weeks after the tournament, Billy Wolfe married Nell Stewart in New Mexico. As a wedding gift, and a consolation prize for her loss in Baltimore, Nell defeated Ida Mae Martinez in Cincinnati for the third annual WLW-TV Championship before a crowd of 16,000 fans. She received a gold belt, $2000, and a portion of the gate. Nell was also named the Texas Women's State Champion.

She was a champion.

But she would never be *the* champion.

Ida Mae Martinez, who was Nell's best friend, later confirmed that the switch had been made because of Burke. "[Billy and Nell] were really ticked off because Nell was supposed to be the champion. Many times, when I think about it, I wish she had been, because her life went downhill after that."

You'd have to be a true, cold-hearted cynic not to feel at least something for Nell Stewart. All those years of paying her dues, putting Mildred Burke over, and giving Billy Wolfe whatever he wanted. Burke played spoiler, her poison telegram ruining what was to be Nell's grand coronation.

The history of wrestling is filled with such moments, when an unexpected turn of events threw a wrench into the course of history. The infamous WWF "Curtain Call" on May 19, 1996 in Madison Square Garden, when Triple H, Scott Hall, Kevin Nash, and Shawn Michaels broke character to take a bow prior to Hall and Nash's departure for WCW, led to a change at the next WWF pay-per-view. Triple H was slated to win the 1996 King of the Ring, but Vince McMahon decided to make an example out of him.

Triple H went on an inglorious losing streak. Steve Austin won King of the Ring, coined the phrase "Austin 3:16," and became one of the biggest stars in the business. Triple H's career recovered, but his moment of hubris opened the door for Austin to leap ahead and take his place in history.

A lesser-known but no less impactful branch in the wrestling timeline was chronicled on the wrestling blog Ring the Damn Bell by Brian Damage. Shortly after winning the Intercontinental Championship from Randy Savage at Wrestlemania, Ricky Steamboat told Vince McMahon privately he wanted to relinquish the title. McMahon chose "The Natural" Butch Reed to become his successor, but when Reed was a no-show on the night of the planned switch, McMahon went looking for Plan B.

Hulk Hogan suggested Jake "The Snake" Roberts, the man who nearly a decade later would put Steve Austin over as King of the Ring, but Roberts was also a no-show. Hogan pointed to Wayne Farris, a former Memphis and Stampede star now sporting an Elvis-inspired hair and ring attire as The Honky Tonk Man. Farris was thrilled with the opportunity, but he told McMahon he did not want to be a transitional champion. McMahon agreed. The Honky Tonk Man reigned as IC champion for a record 434 days.

The rise of the Honky Tonk Man to Intercontinental Champion had a ripple effect. Unable to fulfill his promise to put the Intercontinental Championship back on Randy Savage, Vince McMahon switched the planned finale to Wrestlemania IV by putting the World Heavyweight Championship on Savage. That change broke a promise to "The Million Dollar Man" Ted DiBiase, so McMahon created the Million Dollar Belt, the most famous non-title wrestling belt in the world, to appease DiBiase. DiBiase wasn't happy with the decision at the time, but he later confessed that the Million Dollar Belt made him more money than a World Championship ever would have.

The no-show of Butch Reed and the Curtain Call both yielded to positive results for the wrestling business. It's difficult to imagine an alternate timeline where Butch Reed winning the Intercontinental title and Triple H winning the 1996 King of the Ring would have led to greater success for the WWF.

So what about Nell Stewart and June Byers? Was June best for business in the long run? Did her surprise victory and her run as champion sustain the Billy Wolfe empire a little while longer? Would a Nell Stewart victory have allowed Billy Wolfe to keep his stranglehold on women's wrestling? Or was the rise of Moolah, backed by Vince McMahon, Sr., an inevitable shift in the sands?

We'll never know what could have been; only what was. June Byers now held the title of Women's World Champion, a title recognized by the NWA. She was now the top girl working for Billy Wolfe. She, not Nell Stewart, was now on a collision course with Mildred Burke.

TRAINING FOR MILLIE

"World Champion, 1936 to 1953."

The headline on the cover of the NWA magazine with Mildred Burke on the front read like an epitaph. There was no mention of Burke inside the June 1953 publication. Instead, the magazine presented a full story on the Baltimore tournament and the coronation of the new women's champion, June Byers.

June's victory brought her fully into the spotlight. Accompanied by her husband G. Bill, she drove around the country in a lemon-colored Lincoln. June's two Pekingese dogs went everywhere with them. The local press rolled out the red carpet anywhere the new champion traveled. June's smiling face appeared in newspapers and magazines, and she was not shy about staking her claim.

G. Bill and June stole more than a few gags from Billy and Millie's playbook. Like his father before him. G. Bill would prompt June to flex her muscles. June would oblige and invite the reporter to feel for himself.

June was in a position very few wrestlers have ever enjoyed. She was a double champion. She wore the new Women's World Championship title belt around her waist, and she continued to defend the $1000 tag team trophy with Mary Jane Mull. In between singles matches, June would link back up with Mull to work against a number of ladies who had stayed loyal to Wolfe, including Lilly Bitter, Ida Mae Martinez, Cora Combs, Dot Dotson, Ella Waldek, and eighteen-year-old LeeChona LaClaire.

The newly minted champ made her YouTube-famous appearance on *What's My Line* in August of 1953. A bigger thrill for Byers was being a guest on the Jack Paar show. A former stand-up comic, radio star, and game show host, Paar had a half hour talk show on CBS every afternoon at 1 p.m. before becoming the host of NBC's *The Tonight Show* in 1957. He was one of the most popular television personalities of his day.

As one of the faces of women's wrestling, June also appeared in the November 20, 1953 issue of *TV Guide*. A rarity for the time, June's photos were colorized, showing her wearing a purple leotard while demonstrating a back breaker on Betty Jo Hawkins. She also posed, smiling, alongside Hawkins and Nell Stewart.

June played the champion everywhere she went, but not everyone was buying it. Some were downright confused. Many were hearing arguments from both sides, making a case for one or the other.

Tampa Bay Times sports editor Bill Beck was one of those trying to make sense of it all. Beck received word from Billy Wolfe and Ed Contos that June Byers was the new world champion based on her victory in Baltimore. At the same time, he received notes from Burke, Burke ally Cora Combs, and others that Burke had not been present at the Baltimore tournament and was still the rightful champ.

Beck noted that Tampa promoter Pat O'Hara failed to acknowledge June Byers as champion during a January 1954 appearance. Despite O'Hara's silence, Byers made her position clear to everyone.

"I am the world's champ. I can lick Mildred Burke any time, anywhere. I can think of lots of girls who can lick her but she won't get in the ring with them."

Burke was hardly silent on the matter. Having set up a base of operations in Atlanta with Burke-friendly promoter Paul Jones, she called her rival out. "June Byers! I'm the world's champion women's wrestler," she declared in a January 1954 interview. "It's been that way eighteen years, and Byers's claim is a lie. She came by the claim by winning a 'framed up' tournament last April in Baltimore.

"Even then the frame-up didn't work. Byers's win was an accident. It was supposed to be Nell Stewart. I will fight both of them on the same night here in Atlanta, winner take all." Burke went on to say that any winnings she received from this challenge would be donated to charity, a bold move considering Burke was selling her diamonds to make ends meet at the time.

It came as no surprise to anyone, except perhaps Burke, when she defaulted on her loans and lost control of Attractions, Inc. Billy Wolfe was ready to swoop in, assuming the balance of her $30,000 debt and reclaiming control of the company they built together. Burke emancipated herself from the company in the process, refusing to allow Billy Wolfe to handle her bookings, but she was running out of places to work.

Burke had a few allies left in the business. Promoter Jack Pfefer remained in her corner as did Gorgeous George, who gave Burke $4000 cash and told her to "beat that son of a bitch." But other promoters, members of the NWA, stood by Billy Wolfe. Her bookings were being canceled left and right. Her only hope to retain her title, and her standing in the business, was a convincing victory over June Byers.

And there was only one way to get it.

Burke would never allow June Byers to pin her of her own volition, no matter how high the payday might be. Wolfe knew this as well as Burke. He also knew that Burke would never let up on her campaign to be recognized as champion. He had most of the NWA on his side, and some in the media, but until Burke and Byers squared off in the ring, Byers would never fully escape Burke's shadow.

The match would also give both camps something they hadn't seen for a while: a sell-out crowd. In the few places Burke could get work, the crowds simply weren't turning out anymore. June Byers was also not drawing a crowd, in part because so many continued to cast doubt on the validity of her title.

Wolfe was losing money for the first time in years. He was also about to lose his new bride. Before Burke and Byers faced off for the final time, Nell Stewart would leave him for Joe Gunther, an NWA member from New Orleans. Wolfe never stopped loving Nell, but he quickly moved on to another new lover: eighteen-year-old LeeChona LeClaire.

Burke's business partners, Don McIntyre of Atlanta and Cowboy Luttrall of Tampa, proposed a temporary business arrangement between Burke and Wolfe. The idea was for Burke and Byers to go on tour, trading the title back and forth. It looked like a moneymaker on paper, but Burke didn't trust Billy Wolfe not to pull out the moment she dropped the belt to Byers.

Burke let it be known that any match with any wrestler from Billy's camp would be a shoot: a legitimate contest and not a "worked" wrestling match. Burke cut her teeth in the business shooting on local yokels in the carnival, sending many men and women home with very real injuries that convinced them and all bystanders that the rasslin' witnessed under the big top was real.

A champion who could shoot was still seen as a necessity, even in the mid-1950s. The era of double-crosses in the ring was mostly gone, but the NWA still trusted its title to a man in Lou Thesz who could easily defend himself should a wily challenger try to take his belt by force. Burke knew how to defend herself, and she was not afraid of June Byers.

"I was one of her original trainers," Burke wrote. "June Byers was not a particularly good wrestler in the legitimate sense, but she was rough. You always had to watch the dirty punch, dirty knee, and other sharp shots that she took when the chance came."

Burke was nursing a knee injury when she learned that a title match had been scheduled with Byers. The match would be a shoot, two-out-of-three falls, with no time limit. The result would determine once and for all whether Burke or Billy Wolfe would control the women's wrestling business.

The timing for Burke was terrible. The injury in question was an older one that caused her knee to slip in and out of the joint. She needed surgery, but she was struggling so much financially, she had a doctor drain and wrap the knee so she could keep working.

Burke later contended her business partners had conspired against her, choosing that exact moment in time to schedule the match. Strapped for cash, and proud as ever, Burke agreed to the match, now scheduled for August 20, 1954, in Atlanta.

Burke had no way of knowing that June Byers had been training for this match for months. She set up base camp in Columbus Ohio, and Billy Wolfe made it his mission to turn June into Mildred Burke's kryptonite. Wolfe had taught Mildred Burke everything she knew about shooting. Not only would he teach June Byers those same skills, he would teach her every weakness his ex-wife had.

Wolfe also brought in help. Ralph "Ruffy" Silverstein was a collegiate wrestling champion from Illinois. He had never made a splash in the professional ranks because he lacked the showmanship needed to be a star. But what Silverstein lacked in charisma he more than made up for in skill.

"I trained very hard for that bout, seven hours a day, five days a week, running five miles a day," said Byers. "I trained in Al Haft's gym with Bill Miller, Dick Hutton, and Joe Scarpello. Joe in particular I could wrestle with, the others were way too big. I did beat a college wrestler who weighed 189 points, I weighed about 145 at the time. Billy had me train with the men to increase my strength and endurance. When I wrestled my normal matches against women wrestlers I had a definite advantage."

It was during that intense period of training that Joe Louis, the legendary boxing champ, dropped in to watch Byers work out. After observing the lady grappler in action, the legendary boxing champ Louis quipped, "If boxers had the same conditioning program of June Byers, then we'd have a much better game with men getting hurt less. This woman is one of the best trained athletes I ever saw." Louis stayed a week, working out every day with June.

In addition to the heavy training regimen, Byers wrestled a series of "Beat the Champion" matches to further legitimize her status. She sometimes wrestled two or three matches a night during this stretch, both male and female. One of the sacrificial lambs offered up by Billy Wolfe was a St. Louis girl named Mary Ann Kostecki, better known to fans as Penny Banner.

Banner was already working out in the gym, training with

Wolfe, and Byers had already taken notice of her. Spying the new girl while passing through one day, she gave Billy her thoughts. "Look at her thighs and her arms and her hamstrings. She is one powerful girl, and mark my words, she's going to go far."

Banner took note of Byers as well, especially the "diamond as big as a quarter" on the champ's finger. When Billy told Penny about June's open challenge, he urged her to accept. Penny went to the weekly show intending to do just that.

"I don't know what was wrong with me," said Banner in the *Lipstick and Dynamite* documentary. "I said okay, then I said to myself, 'Oh my goodness, she wrestles men, and he wants me to challenge her!'"

Banner was the second person to take June on that evening. A gentleman selected from the crowd lost to June very quickly. By all accounts, even these intergender matches were shoots.

"Penny Banner told me that she watched June defeat a male wrestler in the ring while June was preparing for her match with Mildred in 1954," says Jeff Been. "That's how imposing June was."

After watching June dispose of her male challenger, it was Penny's turn. If Banner was impressed by Byers's stature with her regular clothes on, she was more so when she stepped into the ring and saw June in her ring gear. "I guessed she was 5'6" and about 170 pounds," Banner wrote in her autobiography *Banner Days*. "She had a thick back, very tight and high thigh muscles, big muscular arms and neck. Plus — she had 10 years' experience against my none and looked like a race horse."

Who "won" the match depends on whose version you choose to believe. While Banner certainly didn't claim to have pinned the champ, she did say that she lasted the time limit. It did not happen easily.

"Each time she took me down and got on top of me, I kicked out and ended up under the ropes," said Banner. "She just got up and pulled me back to the middle, not letting me get any breath or rest before she was all over me again. No one had done that to me. I had to be on constant guard to stay off the mat."

When the bell rang, signaling the end of the ten-minute challenge, the referee raised both women's hands. Billy came into the ring and handed her a check for fifty dollars, declaring, "You are now a wrestler."

June told a much different version of the story to Jim Melby in 1984. "I did defeat her in a couple of minutes, but she wasn't convinced of the fact, so I had to beat her two or three more times."

Regardless whose version of history is correct, the respect was there for Banner right from the get go. "After that, [Penny] also trained under Billy Wolfe, and I took her under my wing as a protege. Sometimes I think I trained her too well, as after I became champion, Penny was one of my toughest challengers. She gave me some of my hardest fought matches. I really thought after my retirement that she would emerge as the new champion."

In an interesting bit of timing, the August 1954 issue of *Boxing and Wrestling* magazine ran a story about June Byers. Penned by Carleton Squires, the sub header leading into the story made note of June's determination to "reign as undisputed Women's World Wrestling Champion." As with many articles about lady wrestlers, the story began with a heavy focus on "Diamond" Billy Wolfe and his vast women's wrestling empire before delving into the June Byers backstory. Nevertheless, if Mildred Burke got her hands on a copy prior to August 20, it would have added even more fuel to her fire.

June worked a light schedule of events during the summer of 1954, wrestling ladies who had signed on with Girl Wrestling Enterprises: Mars Bennett, Ella Waldek, Belle Drummond, Violet Viann. She also continued to take challenges from fans, preparing for the challenge ahead.

Mildred Burke worked a lighter schedule leading up to the bout, sticking mostly to the friendly confines of Georgia. She worked August 19 against a friend and ally, Catherine Simpson, in Gainesville, but she canceled an August 17 booking in Louisville to prepare for

Byers. Louisville promoter Francis McDonogh noted Burke was defending against Byers in Atlanta and promised to have the winner at the Columbia Gym within two weeks. It would take seven months to get the winner — and NEW women's champion — to Louisville.

CHAMPION VS. CHAMPION

"Next week's main event will pit World Champ Mildred Burke against June Byers. Burke has never lost a bout."

One paragraph, two sentences. That's all the hullabaloo the biggest match to date in the history of women's wrestling received from *The Atlanta Constitution*. Argentina Rocca headlined the show on August 13, one week before the shoot was to take the place on August 20.

The public had no idea the significance of what was about to happen. For Atlanta fans, it was another Friday night at the fights. Burke had come to town just a week earlier, defeating Bonnie Watson on August 6. Seeing Burke defend her title in two weeks was rare but not outside of the norm.

The contest certainly looked like a mismatch on paper. June Byers had the height and weight advantage. She had ten years of bumps, bruises, and broken bones, but Burke had almost twenty. Burke was also working on a bad knee, a weakness well-known to Byers and Wolfe. She needed surgery, but pride and desperation had kept her from taking time to get it fixed.

Working the injured body part is a regular piece of wrestling storytelling then and now. A grappler like Kurt Angle, for example, would work the lower leg of his opponent over and over, softening him up for the dreaded Ankle Lock. In Byers vs. Burke, this would not be a work. Byers was looking to hurt Burke, to disable her long enough to make her submit.

The "X" Factor was Mildred Burke herself. There's nothing more dangerous than a wounded animal, and Burke was wounded in more than just her physical capacity. Burke felt supremely confident going into the match, and most of the fans were right behind her. Burke had always, always retained her title against June Byers. Always! Why would August 20 be any different?

Mildred Burke also had a clear picture of how June planned to attack and how to counter. June would go for the knee, there was no question, but a young man now working for Burke would give her yet another maneuver to avoid. Bert Younker was a childhood friend of Mildred's son Joe. He was nineteen years old and had taken over the driving duties for Burke from Joe.

Joe, who flew in from California for the match, was in his mother's locker room when Bert walked in with a warning. While walking past the men's locker room, Bert heard some of the boys discussing a move Ruffy Silverstein had taught June. Younker did not get all the details, but he picked up one important note. Mildred had to stay out of the ropes. This special "move" started with putting your opponent into the ropes, and if Burke could avoid that predicament, she could avoid whatever came next.

Sitting in their hot dressing rooms inside City Auditorium, Burke and Byers had plenty to time to think and stay limber. They were the main event on a four-match card. Chief Big Heart defeated Jack Dillon, and in a tag bout, Red and Don McIntyre defeated Jack Steele and El Toro (aka Bibber McCoy). The opening contest saw Wild Bill Zim lose to Dr. Jerry Graham, the younger Vince McMahon's all-time favorite wrestler.

Zim's son Mike Zim has spent years chronicling his father's career. His dad left behind a scrapbook full of amazing photos. Sadly, he never said anything to his son about the night Mildred Burke and June Byers clashed for the last time.

"He didn't talk much about wrestling," says Mike Zim. "He talked more about the military."

The referee entered the ring ahead of the ladies, lending the affair gravitas by his mere presence. Billy Thom was not only a former pro wrestling champion himself, he was a successful college wrestling coach at Indiana University. The Hoosiers were national champions in 1932 under Thom and runner-ups twice to Oklahoma State in 1934 and

1940. Thom's success in Bloomington also gave him the opportunity to coach the 1936 US Olympic team, a team that won one gold medal and three silvers in Berlin.

One of Thom's students at IU was a kid from Hammond, Indiana named Dory Funk. Thom would play a role in helping Dory, best known as Dory, Sr., to launch his own career as a professional wrestler.

All that being said, Billy Thom was part of the Indianapolis booking office at the time and an ally of Billy Wolfe, another card in a deck stacked against Burke.

Billy Wolfe sat next to his new teenage girlfriend Lee Chona LeClaire near Byers' corner. Burke had to take some satisfaction to seeing that he, like her, was no longer decked out with diamonds. When Byers entered the ring and removed her robe, she turned to her son in astonishment.

"Joe," she said, "I can't believe that is the same girl we knew as June Byers."

That was the moment Mildred fully realized how hard June had prepared for this moment. All the push-ups, the back bends, the running. All those nights taking on all comers. Her official weight was typically 150, but Burke believed June had swollen to 180 pounds of pure muscle.

There's no footage of the match that took place that night, and only the barest facts made it into the Atlanta papers the following day. It would take some time before the results of the match were truly "known" and publicized, as things did not go the way Billy Wolfe or Mildred Burke had hoped.

To many who witnessed the occasion, there just wasn't much to write about. Not compared to the "traditional" women's matches fans were accustomed to seeing. Jeff Leen sketches together the most complete version of events in Burke's biography, *Queen of the Ring*, painting a picture of a bout that, in the end, proved to be satisfying to absolutely no one.

With all the build up to the match, anticipation was high the two ladies would pull out all the stops and put on as hard-hitting a match as any ever seen in Atlanta. Imagine the confusion and disappointment in the crowd as the two ladies tossed all hint of showmanship out the door and engaged in the kind of wrestling that once packed the opera houses in the days of William Muldoon and Clarence Whistler.

While Billy Wolfe, G. Bill, Joe, Bert Younker, and others "in the know" at ringside were riveted by every insufferable moment, the crowd grew restless. Locked in a tight collar and elbow hold, June kept trying to get Mildred into the ropes, but the champ used the bigger woman's momentum to swing her around and stay in the center of the mat.

June tried to get to Mildred's knee. Mildred did her best to wear the bigger woman down, to frustrate her, biding her time in the hopes June would wear down or make a mistake. Compared to the slam-bang action both ladies had delivered throughout their career, it was a snooze fest.

The pivotal moment came sixteen minutes into the contest, when Burke went down to the mat. Mae Young, who saw the action from ringside, said Byers tripped Burke and went for the pin. Burke claimed her knee had popped out of the socket and caused her to stumble. Byers went for the pin, and referee Billy Thom counted to three. One fall for June Byers, none for Mildred Burke.

Burke would later claim she "allowed" Byers to pin her, believing she could come back from one fall down and pin Byers twice. It would prove to be her undoing, but in that moment, the match was far from over. Byers had to score a second fall, and with no set time limit, the ladies had all the time in the world.

When the bell rang again, Burke and Byers locked up in the same collar and elbow hold that had begun the match. Byers continued to push Burke to the ropes. Burke continued to pivot, wary of the secret weapon in Byers's arsenal. Neither woman gave an inch. The crowd grew restless, jeering and booing the two women they had come to see flying all over the mat. They ignored the calls to "Do something!" as the room grew more and more restless.

Referee Billy Thom finally took action. Forty minutes after Byers had pinned Burke, he informed the ladies he would call the match if another pin did not happen within five minutes. Burke and Byers continued their war of wills, but five minutes later, Thom made good on his word. He called for the bell, ending the bout at just over an hour.

Burke was furious. In her account, as captured in *Queen of the Ring*, she demanded a microphone and told the crowd she was not done. She would fight all night if that's what it took to retain her title.

"Either we continue the match, or you announce that I'm still champion," she said.

Burke describes June Byers as completely winded and exhausted, with blood trickling from her nose. It's a dramatic depiction of a pivotal moment in wrestling history, a champion denied her moment to prove she was still the queen! But if the ring announcer did indeed declare her to still be champion, word of that declaration did not spread beyond the arena.

The match received barely more than a paragraph in the August 21 edition of *The Atlanta Constitution*, a publication that had given a great deal of coverage to Burke over the previous year. The paper noted that Byers had scored the lone pin fall after sixteen minutes but that the athletic commissioner had stopped the match after forty-five minutes.

There's no mention of a title change, but there's also no confirmation that Burke was declared to still be champion.

The Tampa Times ran a story the same day under the banner, "June Byers Gets 'Moral' Victory Over Miss Burke." The Florida paper noted that Byers scored one fall over the champion but the match, declared a no-contest, was supposed to go for two.

It was said that local promoter Cowboy Luttrall was trying to arrange a rematch in Tampa. "[It was] dull, but it should have been completed," said Luttrall.

Gloria Barratini was less gracious in her review. Fifty years later, she called the match "Stinko." Mae Young agreed. She faulted both women for not at least trying to entertain the fans while settling their differences. Nevertheless, Mae always insisted that June never beat Mildred Burke. She got the single fall when Burke's knee gave out, but she never got the second.

In a truly rare piece of wrestling journalism for the time the *Tampa Bay Times* published a story August 22 that acknowledged while most wrestling matches were scripted, Burke vs. Byers was the real deal.

"Only wrestling insiders know the full story of the bitterness existing between Burke and Byers, the charges that have passed between the two and the story of the Baltimore elimination tournament which Byers won but Burke refused to participate in. For that reason, the Atlanta match was largely unheralded. Few of the unsympathetic patrons realized they were seeing what wrestlers call a 'real shooting match' — one in which there is no script to follow and the best man wins."

Speaking to SLAM Wrestling's Greg Oliver, Beverly Lehmer claimed there was actually a script for the match — at least, one that was proposed to Mildred Burke. "[June] was going take the first fall, and Mildred was going to take the next two. So June Byers took the first fall. In the second fall, June Byers was going to take that too, but Mildred doesn't know that. It lasted an hour and something. The crowd is booing. That isn't professional wrestling because it started to be a wrestling match. They called it. Billy Wolfe went to the AP wire, I guess, and said June Byers won the match, she was now world's champion."

Mildred Burke left the arena in Atlanta with the title belt that bore her image on the front. June Byers also left the arena carrying a championship belt, the one awarded to her a year earlier in Baltimore. In the days to come, it was June's belt that would be elevated in status while Burke's diminished.

The Knoxville Journal in Tennessee was the first newspaper to declare Byers the champion on August 21, the day after the Atlanta match. "June Byers won the world's women's championship here tonight by defeating Mildred Burke, long-time titleholder, in a 48 minute struggle. The new champion used a reverse toehold to finish off her opponent."

The Orlando Sentinel proclaimed the match a draw on Saturday, August 22, but by Saturday the 28th, that same paper was promoting a title match between Mary Jane Mull and the new champion, June Byers. Just ten days after she pinned Burke, Byers defended her new title against her former tag team partner. A day later, she defended the title against Ida Mae Martinez in Tampa.

The June Byers era had begun.

Opinions on the match are as varied today as they were in 1954. Burke diehards insist she never lost the title, but in the end, titles in pro wrestling are decided not by the wrestlers but by the promoters.

June Byers was, by virtue of her 1953 tournament victory, a women's wrestling champion. June Byers had scored a pin fall on the long-reigning champion without being pinned herself. She wrestled more than an hour in a shoot match against the legendary Mildred Burke, taking everything the battered and bruised champion could dish out.

Burke had taken the same from Byers, holding off a woman seven years younger with a decade less wear and tear on her body, four extra inches in height, and as much as forty extra pounds of muscle.

Despite all the controversy, Mildred Burke and June Byers agreed on one thing. To them, it was the greatest wrestling match of their lives.

Taking the bull by the horns — literally. Rare promo pic from grandson Will Byers' collection.

June held the Women's Tag Team Championship trophy first with Millie Stafford…

And then with Mary Jane Mull

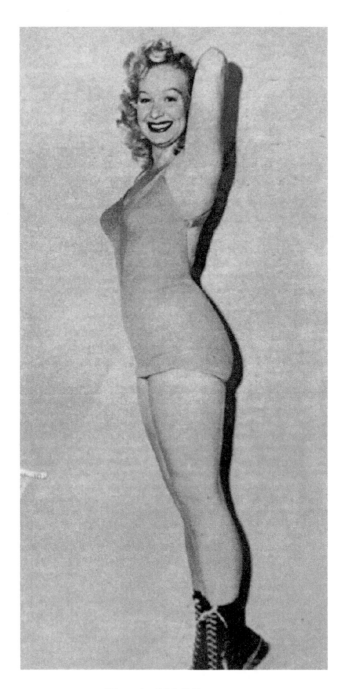

Ring rival Nell Stewart.

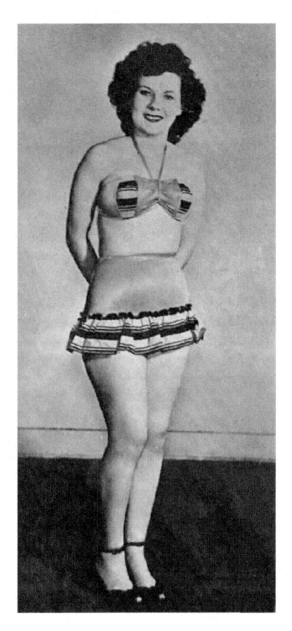

Ring rival and good friend Cora Combs.

June vanquishes barefoot Lily Bitters (top) and Nell Stewart to become champion in Baltimore 1953.

Maryland Athletic Commission Chairman James T. Holmes presents June Byers with her Women's World Championship belt in 1953.

A pair of champions: Lou Thesz and Mildred Burke.

A cartoon celebrating June Byers, Women's World Champion, and her many accomplishments. Courtesy Will Byers.

On vacation: a photo collage of June, her son Billy Boy, and good friend Mars Bennett at the Aquacade. Courtesy Marcella Robinette.

Top: June signed with snapshot with Mars and Billy Boy to Mars. Courtesy Marcella Robinette. Bottom: Penny Banners suffers in the Byers Bridge.

Betsy Ross became Billy Wolfe's secretary, June's valet, and the "Marilyn Monroe" of the ring before becoming Mrs. G. Bill Wolfe. Courtesy Chris Bergstrom.

June shows reporter Roy Thompson who's the boss, 1956.

Promo pic of June with one of her beloved fur babies.

REVISIONIST HISTORY

History is written by the victors. What is true for nations is true for wrestling, especially in the era before cable TV and the Internet.

The December 1963 issue of *The Ring Wrestling* magazine states that the championship belt carried by June Byers was, in fact, the same belt previously carried by past champions Cora Livingston, Clara Mortenson, Barbara Ware, and Mildred Burke. The wrestling fans of the 1960s had no record books and no Internet to check the facts, so the story evolved.

Burke would spend the rest of her life defending her status as champion. The match was never finished. A rematch never took place. Yes, June Byers pinned her, once, but she had to do so twice in order to become champion.

Billy Wolfe had plenty of allies to help him shout down Burke's claim to the title. His allies, eager to keep booking the stars of Girl Wrestling Enterprises, acknowledged June's victory and advertised her as the winner.

Promoting an October 1954 match between June and Betty Jo Hawkins, *The Wichita Eagle* spun the story that Byers had simply worn Burke down and forced her to quit. "It wasn't so much as how Miss Byers came by her title, it was rather her untiring efforts to reach her goal that hot, humid night. In the deciding fall after it had progressed almost one hour and a half. Neither contestant had gained the fall, Miss Byers winning when Miss Burke simply had to surrender to her foe's stamina."

Burke would start another women's wrestling company. She'd train more girls to wrestle. She'd introduce women's wrestling to Japan. She named herself champion of her own company, and when she retired, she retired a champion. She did all this in relative obscurity.

Billy Wolfe and the NWA moved on quickly from Mildred Burke. All the accolades and adoration that used to go to Burke now went to June Byers.

Charles A Smith of *Boxing and Wrestling* magazine did a feature story on rising star Mars Bennett in the December 1954 issue. "Buzz Saw Bennett" was a circus star in the 1940s for Clyde Beatty and then the Ringling Brothers and Barnum & Bailey Circus. She became a pin-up queen, popular with men who liked girls with muscles, and segued into wrestling in the 1950s.

"It was in Sarasota that I first came into contact with Gal Grappling," said Mars in the interview. "June Byers was visiting the Circus winter headquarters. We got together after she had seen my trapeze act, and sold me on gal grappling. I began to practice with any of the girls who were in town. I thought a lot about what June told me, and I was still thinking after I took a bad tumble from the trapeze."

The Bennett legend goes that after recovering from her injury, she left the circus to pursue wrestling full-time. Bennett detailed her early struggles to Smith, saying that her toughest matches to date had been with June and Nell Stewart. Mars began to doubt whether she had what it takes to make it, but she credited the new champion with helping her persevere.

"My good friend, June Byers was keeping an eye on me. She's always in tip-top condition, rates the greatest as a Gal Grappler, and is always willing to help a youngster who is just starting out to win fame and fortune."

Bennett paints a picture of June as both a friend and mentor. "June worked out with me, taught me plenty, encouraged me all she could, had me ringside when she was wrestling. I well remember one of her matches. It began with her opponent slamming her around a couple of times, and I thought she was in for a tough time, but she was just waiting until her adversary dropped her guard... and when she did, the bout was over with June in less than a minute, Since that day, I've patterned my wrestling after June's."

As touching as Bennett's testimonial was, eagle-eyed *Boxing and Wrestling* readers might have felt a bit of déja vu reading the story. This was not the first time the story of Mars Bennett appeared in the pages of Boxing and Wrestling. A feature by Charles A. Smith on the wrestler first appeared in the June 1952 issue. Many of the same photos and anecdotes appeared in both stories, but there was one detail in the Bennett origin story that changed significantly.

"It was in Sarasota, Florida… that I first got in contact with Gal Grappling. I met Mildred Burke who was visiting the winter quarters of the circus."

Mars tells the same story about her injury and her retirement from the circus, but in the 1952 issue it was Mildred Burke who spurred her to success.

"Mildred Burke was keeping an eye on me and kept telling me I had what it took… that I'd make good. Then I saw Mae Weston and Mildred Burke in a tough match. Mildred was bouncing around all over the place but she was biding her time, content to take a beating until Mae Weston dropped her guard for that fraction of a second… and when she did, that was enough. In less than a minute the match was all over and Mae had been body slammed into defeat.

"From that day on," Bennett said, "I patterned my style after Mildred Burke's."

There's one other change of note between the two stories. In the 1952 article, Mars still rates June Byers as one of her toughest opponents, but the other wrestler who gets that nod is not Nell Stewart. It's Mae Young, who had aligned herself with Burke after the split between Burke and Wolfe.

Bennett never married and did not have any children. Her nieces have kept numerous papers and photos from their aunt's remarkable life. Among those photos are some snapshots from an aquacade show Mars attended with June and her son Billy. Mars's mother, who followed her daughter into the circus life, was working for the aquacade, and the lady grapplers can be seen wearing swim suits and having a wonderful time with Billy Boy. By all appearances, the two were good friends.

That being said, it's very unlikely Mars or June had anything to do with this little piece of revisionist history. The fact that both Mildred Burke and Mae Young had been erased from the Mars Bennett story is evidence enough Billy Wolfe was involved in the republication of the Charles A. Smith interview.

To his credit, Smith was one of the most vocal critics of the 1953 Baltimore tournament. Writing in August of 1953, Smith declared, "No tournament can ever determine who is champion unless the title has been vacated by death or retirement, or unless the winner of any tournament meets the champion."

The revisionist version of the Mars Bennett shows that Smith had come around to accepting Byers as champion. What it doesn't reveal is whether Smith was swayed by the Atlanta 1954 result or good old fashioned cronyism.

As easy as it is to get lost in the corruption, the shady dealings, and the old boys club that was the pro wrestling establishment of the 1950s (and let's be honest, many decades after), the women's wrestling scene of the time was, nonetheless, a force for female empowerment. Much as women took the place of men in the factories and offices during World War II, Mildred Burke and her foes seized the main event on the weekly wrestling shows. The alternative, often, was seeing the freaks like the 400+ pound Hippo Wiggins. Who would you rather pay to see go two out of three falls in the smoke-filled arena?

Women remained main event draws though much of the next decade after the war ended, and not just when Mildred Burke was on the card. June Byers, Mae Young, Elvira Snodgrass, Nell Stewart, Mars Bennett, and more continued to steal the show. For many, it was empowering to see women with glamorous looks take to the ring and beat the hell out of each other. That's what drew more and more women to Billy Wolfe's door in Columbus, Ohio.

Despite its popularity, women's wrestling was still banned in many states, including New York. What's more the sport was often ground zero in the crusade for men to "re-take" lost ground from the so-called weaker sex in the wake of World War II. Those who sought to put women back into the kitchens and sewing rooms of America often pointed to the violence and brutality of professional wrestling to say it was incompatible with femininity.

When Jimmy Jemail posed the question, "Do competitive sports tend to make women less feminine in the October 11, 1954 issue of *Sports Illustrated*, June gave him this response. "What is femininity? I have a handsome 10-year-old son. I simply dote on him. I'm a loving wife and a good cook. I wear expensive clothes and luxurious furs. I own a $5,000 Lincoln Capri. Each day I wear diamonds valued at $30,000 because they always look so new. Am I feminine?"

Chicago radio personality Jack Eigen took the case to American wrestler Ralph "Ruffy" Silverstein during an on-air conversation. "How can anybody stand the loss of femininity? Everything looks sloppy about women wrestling. When I watch women I want to see beauty."

Not every man who shared the spotlight with lady wrestlers approved of the sport themselves, but Ruffy Silverstein earned Byers's respect with his response. "If you want beauty for beauty's sale, you'll have to go to Roxy's Theatre. Over at the wrestling arena, you don't attend to watch a beauty contest."

In an editorial titled "Why Women Wrestle" published in *Boxing and Wrestling* magazine in January 1956, Byers took issue with those who felt women didn't belong in wrestling. "Somehow there's a hypocritical notion that women can become almost anything but wrestlers. I doubt as many scalding remarks have been aimed at strip-teasers and infidels among women as they've been aimed at wrestlers."

Byers argued that wrestling was no more savage than factory work, cab driving, or even track and field, comparing a good wrestling match to dancing. "If a girl is not in condition," she said, "She suffers, and doesn't belong in the field. The fittest survive! Isn't this the code existing across most of society these days?"

June praised Billy Wolfe for the way he coached his ladies to present themselves as ladies, to distinguish themselves from those who wrestled the carnivals. As much as Billy's motives were selfish, he fostered an image of a liberated woman in the lady wrestler. It's a dated image, the woman dripping with furs and diamonds who also happens to know how to scrap in the ring, but for the time, it was revolutionary, shocking, and threatening to those who wanted to keep women in the kitchen.

It also can't be ignored, Wolfe broke more than just gender stereotypes. He championed African American women in wrestling, not only bringing them into the business but promoting matches with white wrestlers. June Byers shared the ring with sisters Ethel Johnson and Babs Wingo, ladies who gave Billy Wolfe all the credit for giving them a chance to pursue their own wrestling dream.

June certainly changed some minds on her own, even if the reasons were admittedly superficial. Calgary sports columnist Johnny Hopkins wrote in 1955 that he had always avoided women's athletics, preferring his ladies to be of the "soft, fluffy variety" preferred by most Canadian men. (Gross.) Meeting June Byers changed his mind — to an extent. In Byers Hopkins saw a driven, successful woman at the top of her game, a woman who bucked the image of lady wrestlers being "ill-mannered and unkempt." A woman with charm, beauty, and a hefty yearly salary that afforded her diamonds and furs.

Progress is progress. But even those little steps forward would be undone by the turn of the century.

There's no question women's wrestling suffered setbacks in the United States that mirrored the fight for equal rights. One can only imagine how disgusted June, Millie, Mars, Elvira, and the rest would have felt seeing the "Paddle on a Pole" and "Bra and Panties" bouts of the WWE's Attitude Era. Ask "Princess Victoria" Vicki Otis her thoughts on ladies wrestling in "three triangles and butt floss."

Yet at the same time the WWE was setting a new low for its portrayal of women, the new independent scene was fostering a new equal rights movement. Women of all body types, not just bikini models, were finding acceptance. They demanded the respect of the fans with matches that equaled the men's in both skill and drama.

The WWE finally caught on as well. They hosted an all-women's pay-per-view. They added a women's Royal Rumble. They put women in the main event of Wrestlemania. Not to be out done, the upstart promotion All Elite Wrestling committed right out of the gate to giving women their due on screen, while Impact Wrestling quietly built the best damn women's division in the US.

There's always a chance the pendulum of equality and respect will swing the other way, but today's lady wrestlers are committed to making that an impossible task.

"The suffragettes of old did not boil their campaign down to specific fields," wrote Byers at the conclusion of her essay. "They wanted, I'm sure, the opportunity for women to excel at any task for which they are suited. Today wrestling is one of them."

June would be proud as hell of Lufisto, Kamille Brickhouse, Charlotte Flair, Britt Baker, Jordynne Grace, Mercedes Mone, and all the women fighting to earn the respect of all wrestling fans, men and women.

She would also agree strongly that as far as we have come, there is still work to be done.

A NEW LEAF

"When I defeated Mildred Burke on Aug. 20th, 1954 in Atlanta I received universal recognition," June Byers told Jim Melby in 1984. "I had reached a plateau at that point, but really that wasn't my final goal. I still had the task of staying on top."

June Byers spent almost a decade chasing gold. Like many of her contemporaries, she wanted to be the girl in the right place at the right time to unseat the women who had inspired them all. She'd left everything in the ring in Atlanta. True, she'd failed to get that second pin, but she'd done something Nell Stewart likely could not: she'd avoided taking a single pin from an angry, desperate Mildred Burke.

The target was off Mildred Burke. It was now squarely on the back of June Byers, and the women of Girl Wrestling Enterprises were not the only ones aiming for her. Clara Mortensen, Moolah, and even Mildred Burke herself all wanted a piece of her.

It turned out life on the road was just as precarious as life in the ring. Byers was only two months into her reign when a scary incident happened. The story made headlines across the country and even appeared in the pages of *Sports Illustrated*.

June was traveling home from a show in Kansas City to Columbus. Her husband G. Bill was behind the wheel, driving June and another lady wrestler, when another vehicle with a siren and a flashing red light on top pulled alongside and attempted to force her off the road. Seeing the flashing light, they expected they were being pulled over by the police. Instead, four men wearing masks and carrying guns appeared from the second car. Each of the men wore caps, but the victims described them as being in their late twenties and possibly foreign. Two of the men hopped into Wolfe's car. One of them took the wheel and drove the vehicle to a gravel side road.

The masked men pulled G. Bill from the car and beat him before tying him up. Both of the ladies were tied up as well. The thieves scored big time, taking two diamond rings, a horseshoe stick pin with diamonds and a large ruby, and a watch fob covered in diamonds. All told, the goods were worth $11,500. Wolfe lost $370 cash to the thieves as well.

June had a diamond and platinum ring, a diamond-encrusted watch, and a pair of two carat diamond earrings taken, a haul valued at nearly $10,000. She somehow managed to hide another ring from the thieves, one valued at $7000.

The thieves disconnected the horn and the ignition wires before driving away. G. Bill, June, and their traveling companion managed to wriggle out of their binds and make their way to a farmhouse, where they called for the police.

The papers that identified the third person in the car gave the name Betty Floyd. Fans who had seen her wrestling recently knew her as Betty Jo Hawkins, one of the first women in line to challenge the new champion June Byers. As much as fans felt for the victims of this highway robbery, it would have been bad for business if fans knew it was Betty Jo Hawkins tied up on the side of the road with June Byers.

June faced a number of challengers in the first few months of her reign, from Ida Mae Martinez to Dot Dotson to her former tag partners Mary Jane Mull and Millie Stafford. As champion, however, her greatest rival would be the girl shee'd first grappled while training for Mildred Burke, wrestling's newest blonde bombshell Penny Banner.

One of the best surviving films of Byers and Banner is a newsreel available to watch on the Youtube thanks to Joe Dombrowski's Pro Wrestling Library. The three-minute, black and white clip shows the two ladies exchanging drop kicks, closed fist punches, hard flips, and a brutal knee lift before Byers finishes Banner off with the Byers Bridge. The cameras also captured the many well-dressed ladies in the crowd enjoying the action as much as the men.

Penny Banner would wrestle June Byers more than 120 times in her career, sometimes getting that rare victory in a tag team bout. The best she could ever manage as a single was to take the champion to a draw, something she did March 1, 1955 when the two met in Louisville, Kentucky. Her time as champion would come thanks to another promotion, the American Wrestling Association, and promoter Vern Gagne.

Millie Stafford returned to the fold by the end of 1954 and wrestled her former partner for the Women's Championship. The duo reunited in December for a tag match against new rivals Betty Jo Hawkins and Penny Banner. A month later, they were once again defending their tag titles in St. Joseph, Missouri.

No explanation was given as to how Millie, not Mary Jane Mull, was once again champion alongside June. The St. Joseph fans never heard about the change, so no explanation was needed.

Being the champion brought a change to the way June wrestled, a change that many of her opponents welcomed. "I was so afraid Byers would hammer me with those knee lifts again," wrote Penny Banner about a tag match against the new champ, "But she had changed her style of wrestling, since winning the NWA title from Mildred Burke. She was now wrestling 'clean.'"

The fans in Bismarck, North Dakota didn't notice much difference when Byers faced Banner in January of 1955. A standing room only crowd of over 3100 showed up to watch the ladies upstage the boys in a fight that lasted more than an hour. "If the weather bureau is running out of feminine names for its hurricanes," quipped *The Bismarck Tribune*, "There are some 3100 Bismarck residents who would enthusiastically nominate June and Penny, and get a sincere second from referee Stan Mayslack."

As a champion, June had a platform to do some good in the world. She chose to use that status to promote physical fitness to children. June often spoke to schools and boys and girls clubs, talking about the value of exercise, nutrition, and a healthy lifestyle. She also loved visiting sick children in the hospital, brightening the days of boys and girls who were shocked to see the Women's World Champion walk into their rooms.

When giving interviews, the emphasis for June was on the lady part of lady wrestler. Her marriage to the younger Billy Wolfe was now public knowledge, and the couple painted a picture of domestic bliss, free of headlocks and drop kicks, in an October 1954 interview with the UP's Beatrice Washburn.

"No kidding, she works off all her energy in the ring," said G. Bill. "When she comes home there couldn't be a nicer girl — gentle, fun-loving, easy to please. Even with her biceps and tremendous strength, I bet she's a lot easier to live with than these itty-bitty delicate women who are all nerves and nagging. June never nags. She's a wonderful cook. She loves her home. We have two of them, by the way, one in Houston and one in Columbus, Ohio."

June credited her prowess in the kitchen to a love for food. "Roast beef, macaroni and cheese, plenty of vegetables," she said when asked about her diet. "I got to have my three squares a day to be in top form."

June affirmed her love of food in a 1962 interview with Margaret Crimmins in St. Paul, Minnesota. "My biggest problem is being able to eat enough. You wear off a lot of calories when you're in the ring."

Questions about June's win over Mildred Burke continued to dog the new champion in some towns. Burke refused to go away quietly and was able to bend the ear of more than a few sports writers, making promotion of the new champion difficult. Billy Wolfe doubled down in January 1955 when he shared a Western Union telegram received from Atlanta Athletic Commissioner Howard Haire.

"Am abiding by referee's decision declaring June Byers the winner over Mildred Burke, for the world's championship, held in Atlanta, Ga, on Aug 20th. Byers won only fall of match. Congratulations to the new champion."

At least Byers had a match, and a pinfall, over a champion to legitimize her claim. Two months after the Atlanta telegram hit the papers, promoter Bob Johnston of Portland, Maine, was pushing a women's title match with a champion whose claim on the title was a complete fabrication.

Slave Girl Moolah clearly wasn't buying the Byers over Burke story. Neither was her new business partner Jack Pfefer, one of the few influential men in the business who had sided with Mildred Burke against Billy Wolfe. A Jewish immigrant from Poland with a checkered reputation, Pfefer was building his own small troupe of lady wrestlers that included the bald-headed Lady Angel, Darling Dagmar, and, within a few years, June's good friend Mars Bennett.

The wily promoter saw an opportunity in the Byers-Burke controversy. If Wolfe could convince people Byers was champion after winning one fall out of two in a no contest finish, why couldn't he sell someone as women's champion on a complete fabrication?

If you're gonna tell a lie, tell a big one.

The Portland Press Herald put that bold-faced lie in black and white on March 6, 1955. "Moolah hasn't lost a match in Maine; in fact, she hasn't been pinned even for one fall since pinning June Byers and making her claim to the crown."

Moolah had not wrestled Byers, much less pinned her, since the summer of 1949. But fans in Portland were just as blind to the big picture as the fans in St. Joseph, Missouri who came out to see June and Millie Stafford defend their tag team championship two months earlier.

Moolah posed no real threat to June Byers in 1955. For every promoter willing to do business with Jack Pfefer, there were two who wanted to tar and feather him. What's more, every piece of publicity about Moolah made mention of June Byers. Moolah's claim depended on people believing she'd beaten June Byers, but as any good wrestling promoter will tell you, making mention of your competition always puts the competition first in your customer's minds and you second.

Nevertheless, the tides were changing when it came to women's wrestling. The number of promoters who wanted nothing to do with Billy Wolfe was growing by the day, and Moolah would soon find a new ally. The boss of the World Wide Wrestling Federation, a territory that ran shows from New York down to Baltimore and D.C., would push for change in his native New York and the legalization of women's wrestling in that state in 1972. With his backing, Moolah would become the boss of women's wrestling, controlling the girls wrestling game even longer than Billy Wolfe.

The New York promoter was Vincent J. McMahon.

KICKING THE DOORS OPEN

It was rare for Penny Banner to stand in the same corner with June Byers, but such was the case in March of 1955 when the champion and top contender toured the Southwest. The arch-rivals were pitted against two of Billy Wolfe's newer signees, a pair of sisters who hid their familial connections behind different last names.

Ethel (Wingo) Johnson, Babs Wingo, and Marva (Wingo) Scott were all sisters, born and raised in Decatur, Georgia. The girls followed one another into the business in quick succession. Johnson debuted in 1952 at the age of sixteen and was declared to be "the biggest attraction to hit girl wrestling since girl wrestling began."

Johnson, Wingo, and Scott were part of a trailblazing group of ladies employed by Wolfe in the early 1950s. Their children and grandchildren, some who were featured in Chris Borneau's amazing documentary *Lady Wrestler*, are among the few descendants of Billy Wolfe wrestlers who will sing the man's praises. He gave their mothers and grandmothers an opportunity no one else would. He broke a barrier even more difficult than those broken by Burke and Byers.

They were the first African American ladies to become professional wrestlers.

The Wingo sisters broke more barriers than one with their entry into the business. With only a handful of African American girls available to work, Billy needed them to wrestle against the white and Hispanic girls under his charge. Thus fans were treated to interracial women's matches right from the get-go, with Babs Wingo being the first African American woman to challenge Mildred Burke for the women's world championship on April 28, 1952 in Denver.

Penny and June had their hands full when they faced the Wingo sisters in Arizona, New Mexico, and West Texas. Nell and June

144

were seen as the favorites, but Ethel and Babs were hyped as the "Negro Women's Tag Champions."

After stealing the show from Phoenix and El Paso, June and Ethel Johnson made a little more history. Ethel had wrestled Mildred Burke just once for the Women's World Championship on February 15, 1953. Two years later, on March 29, 1955, she became the first black woman to wrestle for that title in the state of Texas.

The star-packed show also featured Jack Claybourne, a seasoned veteran and one of the first African American men to break out as a star in professional wrestling. Also on hand to referee the main event: the former heavyweight boxing champion Joe Louis.

When June arrived at the Coliseum on March 29, one of the men she shook hands with was Sam Menacker. A former minor league catcher, Menacker turned to the wrestling game after struggling in the New York Yankee farm leagues. His given name was Frank Menacker, but when he started working on camera as an announcer, he changed it to Sam because promoters didn't think Frank sounded Jewish enough.

Menacker organized a studio wrestling show, one of the first, at KROD Channel 4 in El Paso. Through his connections, he booked the biggest stars in the country. He set a local box office record when he booked Baron Leone and Lou Thesz, drawing 7000 fans and grossing $17,000. Sam also appeared in a number of feature films. His most famous appearance was a bit role in the movie *Mighty Joe Young* in which he ripped a phone book in half.

On the March 29 show, he was booked in the main event on February 15, teaming up with Hombre Montana against the dastardly duo of Dirty Don Evans and Larruping Lou Plummer. Sam and Hombre Montana were said to be working out daily at his home and the local YMCA in preparation for what was expected to be a grudge match — hence the reason Joe Louis was called into service.

Byers was still traveling with her husband G. Bill at the time, but the marriage was far from the picture of 1950s bliss painted in the papers. G. Bill struggled with his drinking, and June was reaching the breaking point. Sam Menacker caught her eye, and that connection would soon blossom into much more than a business relationship.

In the Spring of 1955, June and Nell Stewart, now legally the former Mrs. Billy Wolfe, found themselves partners in an unlikely situation outside the ring. The newly elected Democratic governor of Pennsylvania, George M. Leader, appointed three new members to the state's athletic commission with the task of cleaning up the sport of boxing in that state. James Crowley, one of the famed "Four Horsemen" of Notre Dame football, became chairman of the committee that also including Pittsburgh attorney and sports writer Paul Sullivan and Philadelphia attorney and newspaperman Alfred M. Klein.

The commission moved swiftly to enact new regulations on both boxing and wrestling, requiring participants of both sports to submit fingerprints, take out insurance policies, and notify the state of any criminal charges brought against them.

Also on the agenda: a total ban on women's wrestling in the state of Pennsylvania.

Philadelphia promoter Ray Fabiani had asked the commission to allow him to book Byers and Stewart for a match on March 17. When the commission denied his request, Fabiana joined forces with the ladies to file a lawsuit, claiming that by banning women's wrestling, the commission was prohibiting Byers, Stewart, and other ladies from earning a living in Pennsylvania. The ladies had allies in the Philadelphia House of Representatives as well. Rep. Francis X. Muldowney, also a Democrat, introduced a bill in the House that would strip the commission of its authority to put a ban on women's wrestling.

The House measure failed in a 99-82 vote, but the lawsuit moved forward. Calling his challenge a matter of equality between the sexes, Fabiani hired female attorney Sara Duffy to represent himself, Byers, and Stewart.

The Commission didn't seem threatened by the legal challenge. "We're happy to have the suit," said Chairman Crowley after attending a church breakfast on Palm Sunday. "This is the first real test against us. We've only been in office for a month, and we're welcoming our first fight."

The legal challenge in Pennsylvania failed, but doors open in a few places that had long barred women's wrestling. On April 15, 1955, June Byers and Penny Banner became the first women to wrestle in Indianapolis. Promoter Billy Thom, the referee from the Burke-Byers match in Atlanta, booked the girls at the Indiana State Fairgrounds Coliseum where June successfully defended her title.

The Indianapolis Star sports reporter Al Roche shared his thoughts a few days after the bout. "Much of their routine was a carbon copy of the tactics displayed by the male grunt and groan artists, but it was refreshing because of the newness of feminine flippers here."

Roche felt that having women's wrestling too frequently would be too much. That being said, "For occasional entertainment I'll say the women make the men look like a bunch of bums, which many of them are."

Just west of Indiana, another door opened in the summer when Illinois Supreme Court overturned the state's ban on women's grappling. The ban was put into place in December of 1953 by Illinois Athletic Commission at the request of Governor William Stratton. Chairman Livingston Osborne was only too happy to oblige. Such bans were often knee jerk reactions to a single event that someone, somewhere, found offensive. Politicians, then as now, are always happy to capitalize on voter outrage.

A female grappler from Iowa named Rose Hesseltine, who wrestled as Rose Roman, filed a suit against the State of Illinois challenging the ban. The Athletic Commission argued that the ban was an attempt to protect the fragility of women, but Cook County Circuit Judge Harry M. Fisher ruled in favor of Hesseltine.

State Attorney General Latham Castle demanded a rematch, and the State Supreme Court agreed to take up the case. Six months later, the Illinois Supreme Court handed a decisive victory to Rose Roman. Justice Ray I. Klingbell, who wrote the majority opinion, stated that the Illinois Athletic Commission had overstepped its bounds in prohibiting women's wrestling. Only the state legislature, Klingbell wrote, could create such a rule.

China Mira and Dot Dotson had the honor of becoming the first women to wrestle in the newly opened state on July 8 at the Rainbo Arena in Chicago, with Mira getting the win. They were followed by a tag match in which Millie Stafford and Penny Banner defeated Mae Weston and the new Mrs. Billy Wolfe, LeeChona LeClaire.

June had wrestled in Illinois before, grappling with Lillian Ellison at the Harrisburg County Fair in 1948, but she made her Chicago debut with Mae Weston in the Rainbo Arena on July 29. A crowd of 1529 paid $2600 at the gate to see Byers put the Women's World Championship on the line, a drop from the 1738 in attendance for the first night of women's wrestling in the state.

June was still a main event player, and promoters still hyped her as an attraction, but the harsh reality was women's wrestling was still declining in popularity. With Mildred Burke fading into obscurity and other popular stars retiring, Wolfe had fewer stars to push. He continued to train and unleash new, younger women on the ring, but aside from Penny Banner, few had the star power and talent to become an attraction.

June spent more and more time working with Penny and Betty Jo Hawkins as 1955 rolled on, working exclusively with those two in late November and all of December. In January she went on the road with Cathy Branch, a 138 pound blonde billed from Syracuse, Ohio. During a visit to Gastonia, North Carolina, the ladies caught the eye of columnist Bill Williams. A beloved figure in Gastonia who went on to become editor of *The Gazette*, Williams was known for his candor and humor. His colleagues used to joke that you didn't dare mention anything about life outside the newsroom because Bill was likely to write it into his column.

Williams took his two-and-a-half-year-old boys Tommy and Ben to the matches for the first time that night, "a mistake I'll be a long time erasing." The girls were not solely to blame for Williams calling his parenting choice a mistake, but they definitely played a role.

"Everything worked out fine until Tommy began yelling for the Blonde Bombshell Cathy Branch and Ben started rooting for the champ June Byers. One time Tommy figured his gal was getting too many fouls and he let his emotions overrun his better judgment. He grabbed Ben with a Spread Eagle, and Ben countered with a Half-Wrist-Lock-And-Neck-Break."

Williams noted it was the first time his boys had ever seen ladies fighting, but the idea quickly became firmly imprinted on their young minds. When the boys arrived at home, they greeted their mother not with kisses but a Half Nelson.

WHATEVER HAPPENED TO G. BILL?

A smiling June Byers appeared on the bottom of page seven in the January 7, 1956 edition of *The Sentinel*, cinching the waistband of a man in a shirt and tie. The Winston-Salem paper shared the news that a wager had been made between the champion and Mason Bliss, the public relations director for the Memorial Coliseum pictured along with her.

Bliss and Byers got into a discussion about diet and exercise, and when Bliss expressed his desire to lose a few pounds, Byers made him a bet. June taught him her daily exercise regimen and challenged him to do the same exercises every day for two weeks. If he did so and did not lose seven inches off his waist, Byers would pay him a dollar.

If a follow up story in the January 15 edition of the *Journal* is any indication, June had to cough up the dollar. When asked about his progress, Bliss told the *Journal* he had done the exercises and gained two pounds.

Roy Thompson, an award-winning columnist who loved a good smoking pipe as much as a good story, enjoyed some facetime with the champion during her stop in Winston-Salem as well. While speaking about the traditional roles of men and women, Thompson asked June what advice she'd give to a lady who wanted to get married to a man who seemed less inclined.

"The way to a man's heart is through his stomach. I would suggest a knee to the stomach. That's a good way to convince a man that the girl knows best.

"If he is the shy and timid type, a hammerlock might do the trick.

"Once the hammerlock is set, she can also ask him does he love her, and he doesn't dare say he doesn't because she can tear his arm off.

"When she makes him say he loves her, then she can ask him does he want to marry her. He doesn't dare say, 'No.'"

Thompson asked, "But what if the man doesn't want to go to church?"

June turned to size up the writer. "Take you, for instance. Say I wanted to take you to the preacher. If you had longer hair, I could drag you. But men are wearing their hair shorter these days. I guess I'd have to carry you."

Thompson laughed out loud, and June made him regret it. While trying to picture a woman carrying a man, June demonstrated how it's done, yanking Thompson off the ground and over her shoulders into a fireman's carry.

"A man's place is in the home, Miss June Byers said," wrote Thompson. "And Miss June Byers is just the gal who can put a man there. One way or another."

Once Thompson had his feet on the ground, he asked June if she'd ever been married. June said yes, and as a matter of fact, her attorney was drawing up divorce papers to end her current marriage.

"Did you get YOUR husband this Cavewoman way?"

"No," she replied. "I got mine with a rump roast, mashed potatoes, gravy, and a good salad."

The marriage in question, of course, was with G. Bill Wolfe, the man who had sung June's praises and vouched for her own qualifications in the kitchen. As cheery as she made it sound, things were never great for the couple. G. Bill's alcoholism became such a problem, June finally had enough. She had him committed for treatment.

While June has often received credit for pushing G. Bill to turn his life around, a young woman trailing in her shadow deserves far more. Just a few years prior, her father had called Billy Wolfe, Sr., in a moment of desperation. His name was Leland, and his wife had left him high and dry with a house full of children. Leland saw one of Billy's ads in a newspaper, looking for pretty, single girls who wanted to be a wrestler. His oldest child, Betsy, was only fifteen, but she was whip smart and might make a good secretary. Would Billy possibly be able to do anything for her?

Just as he had done with young Janet Wolfe, Billy became Betsy's legal ward, though he wisely kept this a secret after the Janet Wolfe tragedy. Betsy went to work in Billy Wolfe's office, and she got to know all the girls, from Billy's daughter Violet Viann to Karen Kellogg, who became a very close friend. Not surprisingly, she found Mildred Burke to be cold and rough.

Billy was struck by Betsy's beauty, and he soon decided she needed to train to become a wrestler. After teaching her a few basics, he asked June to become her training partner.

Betsy adored June Byers from the moment they met. She went out on the road as June's valet. She helped June get dressed, walked to the ring with her, and held on to her robe and belt at ringside. She assisted June away from the ring as well.

Whenever they had an opportunity, June pulled Betsy into the ring for some training. She did not go easy on her. "Mom says June kicked her ass all the time," says Betsy Wolfe, Betsy and G. Bill's youngest daughter. "But Mom loved her. She never had a cross word to say about June, ever."

June taught Betsy how to fix her hair and makeup and helped her shop for the right clothes. She taught Betsy how to pose for promotional photos. Her youngest daughter has a photo of Betsy Ross dressed in one of June's outfits, posed exactly how June taught her.

"If you look at my mom's wrestling photos, she looks just like June because she poses the same way June does," says Betsy Wolfe.

Betsy was too young to set foot in the ring legally, but once Billy decided she was ready, she did it anyway. For three years straight, she was billed as an eighteen-year-old sensation. Billy had her bleach her hair blonde and promoted her as the Marilyn Monroe of the mat.

June was ringside for several of Betsy's earliest matches. Betsy Wolfe recalls a story her mother told about a match that didn't go quite as planned. "I can't remember who Mom was wrestling, but the girl went off script and getting rough. June was sitting ringside in a strapless dress, her hair and makeup perfect, a mink draped over the back of her chair, just dripping with jewels. She was on the edge of her seat, screaming at this other girl.

"My mom was wearing these wire hoop earrings. I don't know why. But the other girl grabbed one and yanked it, ripping it right through her ear. June screamed at my mom, 'Kill that girl!' My mom socked her right in the jaw and knocked the girl out. June took her out for steak after."

Betsy got to know G. Bill in her travels as well. She saw the frustrations June had with her husband's drinking, and yet in spite of his faults, Betsy developed a crush on him. She kept it secret for fear of offending June. She was G. Bill's wife, after all! But while June, as the wife, was the one who had G. Bill committed for treatment, it was Betsy who spent most of the time at his side, caring for him.

June was already contemplating divorce before G. Bill began his recovery. She'd fallen in love with Sam Menacker, and she was ready to move on. Still, Betsy found it hard to talk to her mentor, her idol, about her feelings for G. Bill.

June was no fool. She could see the way Betsy looked at G. Bill, the way she tended to him during his recovery. Prior to the divorce, June sat down with Betsy.

"I'm not with him for a reason," June said. "I don't love him right now. And if you guys can have a life together, cool."

June gave Betsy and G. Bill her blessing to marry after the divorce became final. She not only gave them a wedding gift, she gave Betsy a small item from one of her own fancy dresses to include in her wedding outfit.

"They remained friends," says Mickie-Mae Johnson, G. Bill and Betsy Wolfe's older daughter. "There was no animosity between June or Mom or G. Bill. Mom was always very fond of June."

G. Bill took control of his addiction to alcohol. He became a born-again Christian and joined Alcoholics Anonymous. He married Betsy and adopted her son William. Betsy had been married very briefly to a Mexican wrestler, and William, it was believed, was the result of that very brief union.

G. Bill and Betsy bought a home in Granville, Texas. They had a daughter, Mickie-Mae, and a son, John. When John was born, Betsy finally hung up her boots to become a full-time mom.

G. Bill got out of the wrestling business right away. He began selling insurance, and while he traveled Monday through Friday, he lived for the weekends when he came home to his kids.

"Dad and I had a tradition," says Mickie-Mae. "When he came home on Friday's, I would jump into his arms and say, 'Daddy, I love you big as the sky!' It was a reference to his favorite song 'Running Bear' recorded by Johnny Preston."

G. Bill mowed the grass and grilled steaks every weekend. His drink of choice became the grapefruit-flavored soda Squirt, and he loved potato chips and vanilla ice cream. He made sure his family went to church every Sunday morning, but he never went into church with them. He'd drop them at the door and pick them up after service.

He never told anyone why he did not attend services, but his children have no doubt he was a man of strong faith. Years after his death, Betsy Wolfe found a box filled with postcards he'd written to Betsy from the road. These very personal messages were filled with love and peppered with the gospel as G. Bill understood it.

"He was praying for her," says Betsy Wolfe. "He was praying for all of us. It felt as if each one of those postcards as a prayer for his family."

Betsy Wolfe never knew her father. She was just nine months old when G. Bill had a heart attack. While waiting for the ambulance, he stunned his children by telling each of them "Goodbye."

"Dad never said goodbye," says Mickie-Mae. "It was too final. He always said, 'So long.' When he said goodbye, I think he knew."

G. Bill also told William he was the man of the house. He

boarded an ambulance and was taken to the hospital where he spent the next eleven days.

"The heart attack he had was one they could easily treat today," says Mickie-Mae. "When he had a second heart attack, my mother knew, even before the hospital called."

Betsy rushed to be by her husband's side. She was already grieving the loss of Billy Wolfe, Sr., who had passed away just a year earlier. They were the two most important men in the young mother's life. G. Bill passed away in her arms that night, and her world, as she knew it came to an end.

The family went through some struggles in the coming years. Betsy, who may well have had some form of mental illness, struggled with grief and made a number of costly decisions. She had another child with a man she dated only briefly. She lost the house in Granville, and for a short time, lost custody of her children. Mickie-Mae found herself taking on the role of mother for her siblings and, at times, for her own mother.

Fortune smiled on the Wolfe family when Betsy Ross met a man named Jim Wilson. Jim loved Betsy, and he was wise enough to know he could never replace G. Bill. When Jim and Betsy married, he hung a portrait of G. Bill, Betsy, and the three oldest children in the hall. He was the husband and father the family needed.

As the years went by, the prayers G. Bill offered for his family began to be answered. Mickie-Mae became a born-again Christian. So did Betsy, thanks to her sister. They prayed with each of their siblings to receive Christ, and that faith G. Bill hoped his family would receive continues to spread to the next generation and the next.

Betsy, who was raised Catholic, never understood her husband's faith until the very end. She was diagnosed with cancer, and one night, she asked Mickie-Mae and Betsy to watch *The Passion of the Christ* with her. The daughters watched as their mother sobbed. Everything G. Bill had shared with her finally clicked. She became a Christian weeks before her death. Her widower Jim Wilson also received Christ shortly before he died.

"It all goes back to my Dad," says Mickie-Mae. "He was praying for all of us, even Jim Wilson."

G. Bill may only be a small, supporting role in the stories of June Byers, Mildred Burke, and Billy Wolfe, Sr., but the faith and love of G. Bill remains the heart of the Wolfe family which is now welcoming a fourth generation into the world. In time, Mickie-Mae's grandbabies will come to know of the tradition she and her father established so many years before.

"I love you big as the sky has become a family thing," she says. "I didn't say those words for years after Daddy died. Then one day, they just slipped out when I was talking to my husband. It surprised even me, and I told him the story. My husband loves abbreviation, so it's become ILYBATS."

Betsy Wolfe and her kids adopted the family code as well, "When we send each other letters or cards, we write ILYBATS on the outside of the envelope. We even use it in texts and emails. My phone knows it so well, it comes up on my auto-correct."

INDEPENDENT CHAMPION

As the 1956 Olympics approached, the sports media in the US began asking the question, how are we going to beat the Russians? Wrestling journalist Charles Smith had a suggestion for the Olympic committee. "I am informed that the Russians pile up a tremendous amount of points with their women's field team and both men's and women's gymnastics entries. Well, I know where the talent is to beat them."

Smith's solution: the Lady Angel, a bald-headed woman who was then a major attraction for Jack Pfefer; and the women's world champion, June Byers.

"They could take care of the field events by themselves," boasted Smith. "June Byers is the strongest woman in the world. She has unlimited stamina. She weighs in at 140 pounds of solid muscle. She can pick up an opponent, lift her solidly over the head and then heave the girl into the third row, ringside.

"Give her a chance at the shot put or the javelin and she is likely to throw the thing out of sight. I know Russia doesn't have a girl who can compete with her."

Sports editor Tom Kinney of *The Columbus Ledger* in Georgia had a different career path in mind for the champion. Citing her movie star looks, Kinney asked Byers if she'd ever considered giving up the ring for acting. June rolled with it, telling Kinney she was glad he had asked.

"I certainly have considered acting. And you'd be surprised how much we wrestlers have to act. Don't misunderstand me. Acting is only a small part of wrestling, but it's necessary. A dead-panned wrestler who never showed any pose and acting ability would never get ahead."

It's as close to breaking kayfabe as a wrestler of her era would dare get. "Acting in wrestling is nothing but good showmanship," June adds. "You notice showmanship in baseball players, boxers, football players, in fact all athletics."

Anyone who watched Reggie Miller do a flop against the Knicks back in the 1990s would have to nod in agreement.

Circling back to the heart of Kinney's question, June adds, "Yes, I've considered acting, but wrestling is more steady."

Just how steady is a question many lady grapplers were struggling to answer. June was still getting premiere bookings like the 1956 Kentucky Derby Eve show in Louisville, but if you weren't the champion, or Penny Banner, or even Nell Stewart, it was getting to be tough going.

A scary incident took place on July 7 when June was wrestling in Medicine Hat, Alberta, Canada. A fan tossed a bottle into the ring and struck the champion in her right eye. As always, Sam Menacker had his wife's back. He spotted the culprit from ringside and plucked Fred Bintz out of his seat so he could be handed over to the police.

Doctors checked June out on site. She suffered hemorrhaging behind her right eye and lost sight temporarily in that eye. She received three stitches and was ordered to spend a few days in bed recovering. Four days later she was back in a Vancouver ring, ready to take on young Bonnie Watson.

Stu Hart was the man in charge of the Alberta territory, and in the summer of 1956, he decided to create his own women's tag team titles. Penny Banner and Bonnie Watson, who conveniently had brought matching outfits on the trip north, were chosen to be the champs while Mars Bennett would tag up with June Byers to chase them.

Banner and Watson were booked as the babyface team, getting the win over June and Mars every night. But when it came time for Penny to wrestle June for the title, June still won every time.

Bonnie and Mars (working as Lois Johnson) created some

fireworks in Nanaimo, British Columbia when they faced one another for the right to wrestle June Byers for the championship. The girls put on a hell of a fight, gouging and kicking and biting. And that's just what they did to the poor referee who was trying to keep order. When Bonnie trapped Mars between the ropes and refused the referee's command to stop drop kicking her, the ref disqualified Bonnie and gave the win to Mars.

This set Mars off even more. She pushed the ref away when he attempted to raise her hand and demanded a microphone. Mars said she didn't want to face June Byers after winning on a disqualification. She wanted to beat Bonnie first and beat her bad!

Bonnie tore after Mars, and a stream of male wrestlers emptied the locker room to separate the girls. It took nearly thirty minutes to restore order, with the referee dragging Bonnie by her blonde locks back to the locker room. Fans were starting to leave when the girls went at it again, this time attacking one another in the hallway. It took the Mighty Ursus, a 320 pound giant, and his 220 pound Ken Kenneth to finally separate the women from one another.

The result of the night? The girls would face each other one week later for the right to wrestle June. Who wouldn't want to come back and see the rematch after such a melee?

The ladies continued their feud when they crossed back over into the states. Watson and Banner remained champions in Arizona, but in Las Vegas and New Mexico, June and Mars were presented as tag champs. In Albuquerque, the *Tribune* sent award-winning columnist and photographer Beverly Wilkinson to the matches to get a "woman's view" of wrestling for once. While Wilkinson admitted to viewing wrestling as "an art or more feinting than fighting," she was impressed by the way the wrestlers, male and female, gave the crowd a night of pure entertainment.

Wilkinson interviewed June Byers, and the big question on her mind was simply, "Why?" June gave the answer she always gave: money! She was making around $30,000 that year, enough to mend any number of broken bones and buy a lot of ice cream sodas for her son

Billy.

Sam Menacker chimed in and assured Wilkinson it wasn't all about the money. Deep down, June loved her work.

June and Mars Bennett were both featured in a publication launched in 1956, *Girl Wrestlers*. Issue one of the new magazine promised readers 137 "sizzling uncensored pics" featuring June, Mars, Penny Banner, Belle Star, Babs Wingo, LeeChona LeClaire, Moolah, and more. Credit the magazine's editorial staff for not choosing sides in the battle for women's wrestling raging at the time. Readers got a glimpse of Billy Wolfe's girls as well as Moolah's girls, the African American ladies of the time, and independents. June received a one page article in addition to three pages of action photos, all under the headline, "Queen of the Glamazons."

June teamed up with Herb Welch, the Southern Junior Heavyweight Champion, in September for a true rarity for the time, a mixed gender tag match. The rules for such a match stated that only men could wrestle men and women could wrestle women. If a partner tags out, then both combatants must step out of the ring and allow the team members of the other gender to take the ring.

Roy Welch and Nick Gulas promoted the show in Birmingham, and over 6000 fans turned out on September 3, 1956. June and Herb had their hands full facing Karl Kowalski and his wife Carol. Of course the champion was not going to take a loss, so it was up to Herb Welch, trainer of Dr. D David Schultz, to get bloodied up and pinned by Karl Kowalski. Fans chased Mr. and Mrs. Kowalski back to their dressing rooms, trying to exact a pound of flesh on behalf of Herb and June.

A month later, the entire wrestling world was shaken when the federal government filed an anti-trust suit against the National Wrestling Alliance. Attorney General Herbert Brownell's suit alleged that the NWA members had created a monopoly by agreeing to respect one another's borders, require members to book only wrestlers connected to the NWA, and blackball anyone who worked for a non-NWA promoter, all of which was true.

Billy Wolfe made light of the suit when asked for comment.

Noting he was only an "honorary member," as the NWA did not officially recognize women's wrestling, Wolfe said the suit left him puzzled. "What in the world would the government want to bother June Byers for? Don't they know how tough she is?"

Wolfe's bravado hid his own fears that his time in the sun was over. Nell Stewart came back to work with him, despite their messy divorce and her personal disdain for the man, but it was purely a business decision. But while Billy Sr. was grateful to have his Betty Grable back, he'd soon lose June for good. Sam Menacker had all the connections June needed to stay busy. She no longer needed Billy Wolfe.

Sam and June returned to Calgary in early 1957. The two of them sat down for a conversation at Stu Hart's hillside mansion along with Stu, Penny Banner, and with *Calgary Herald* writer and cartoonist Gorde Hunter. While Hunter often criticized the "obvious flim-flam of professional wrestling," he held those who put on such entertaining exhibitions in high regard.

"Wrestlers are among my favorites of the sporting world. They are, for the most part, intelligent (far above the sporting IQ average), business men, and what's more important in my business, colorful raconteurs."

Wearing horn-rimmed glasses and smoking a meerschaum pipe, Menacker held court for much of the conversation. He bragged on the travel the women endured, which he said was much more extensive than most of the men. He also spoke about his time as the man holding the atomizer, spraying the ring with Chanel No. 10 for Gorgeous George, and how much happier he was working with his wife. "I'll stick to managing June — it's much easier on my nerves."

Penny Banner and June Byers spoke about their training regimens and the injuries both had suffered. June made mention of the bottle incident a year earlier in Medicine Hat, while Penny proclaimed Jacksonville, Florida to be "the worst place in the world to wrestle. I hate having to appear there."

June appeared on more and more shows that also featured

Sam. If he wasn't wrestling, he was a guest referee. If he wasn't in the ring at all, he was likely ringside, cheering on the champion. He was by June's side when *Fort Lauderdale News* women's reporter Arline Horne timidly approached the door of her dressing room after seeing June dismantle Theresa Theis.

"Without a doubt — this was the strongest, most cat-like and unrestrained woman in the world." At least that's what Ms. Horne believed, until the door opened and the strong scent of lady's perfume wafted into her nostrils.

There sat June, penciling in her eyebrows while two Pekingese dogs named Sundown and Moonbeam wagged their tails in greeting to the stranger.

"Oh don't look surprised, honey," said June in her Texas twang. "Just because I'm rugged doesn't mean I have to look rugged."

June teamed up with Mars Bennett in Tennessee for some tag team action as well as a few, final clashes for the Women's World Championship. Like June, Mars Bennett also went rogue, parting ways with Wolfe to take bookings from Jack Pfefer. While breaking away from Billy Wolfe meant she was keeping more money from her payouts, a letter Mars sent to Jack on May 28, 1957 indicates just how tough it could be for a lady wrestler at the time.

"Dear Bundles Sugar-Daddy Jack, Just a few lines to let you know everything is fine. Only no Bundles. This territory is really bad."

On a summer afternoon in Nashville on August 23, 1957, Mars Bennett hopped in the station wagon she owned with partner Belle Drummond. Young Belle Starr was riding shotgun, and hefty wrestler Larry Clark took the backseat. The three were headed for Greenfield, Tennessee, but they barely made it out of Nashville before being struck head-on by a cement truck.

People who witnessed the accident were shocked to find any survivors. Belle Starr was thrown through the windshield but alive. Clark was alive as well, but trapped in the backseat. Both Starr and Clark were badly injured.

Mars was crushed between the driver's seat and the steering wheel. She was dead on impact.

Belle Starr and Larry Clark didn't know she had passed until the next day. The news spread slowly throughout the wrestling community.

Mars was scheduled to wrestle in Tampa the following week against Verne Bottoms, with the winner receiving a title shot against June Byers. Instead, a grieving Belle Drummond had to make the long drive south to wrestle Verne Bottoms in her partner's place.

June's grief was near that of Belle's. Mars had been a favorite opponent and tag partner in the ring and that rare thing outside the ropes: a dear friend. Her loss, at the age of thirty-five, was a shock. Everyone who wrestled for any length of time knew someone who had suffered in a car accident. Some, like Mildred Burke and Belle Starr, were fortunate enough to recover and get back on the road. Some survived but were never able to wrestle again, like Elvira Snodgrass and Larry Clark.

And some, like Mars Bennett, were lost too soon.

REIGNING AND DEFENDING

Finding some sense of stability with Sam Menacker, June began to cut back on her bookings in 1957. While the numbers on Wrestlingdata.com are far from complete, they paint a fairly accurate picture of the slowdown. After wrestling 122 matches in 1954, 123 matches in 1955, and 141 matches in 1956, June went to 78 in 1957. The coming years would see her wrestling even less, a change that let June catch her breath while others moved in to seize control of women's wrestling.

You can hardly fault June Byers for the change in power that took place. She'd given her body and mind and soul for professional wrestling for thirteen long, grueling years. She had earned the title by her hard work, in and out of the ring. She would spend the rest of her days in the ring as an attraction, the woman who unseated Mildred Burke, the reigning, defending Women's Champion.

The Menackers spent November in Calgary working for Stu Hart, where both Babs Wingo and Ethel Johnson faced June for the Women's World Championship. After a few weeks in Tennessee in early December, where one of June's opponents included Elvis's latest fling Penny Banner, the couple returned to the Great White North to ring in the New Year.

Byers could still draw a crowd in Canada. In the dead of winter, January 16, 1958, more than 4700 fans braved the bitter cold to see June defend the title against Canadian Alma Mills in Regina, Saskatchewan.

Stu Hart was good to June, and June was a regular in Calgary throughout the rest of her career. Stu loved hosting June during the Stampede, the largest annual festival in Calgary that included a rodeo, parade, and special events including — what else? — professional wrestling. While others were happy to move on to Moolah, Stu hailed June as the Women's World Champion until she retired.

The fewer bookings June took, the more of a special attraction she became. Some promoters took the opportunity to schedule her with old rivals like tag partner Millie Stafford, Gloria Barratini, Betty Jo Hawkins, and a woman who wrestled well into her 80s, Mae Young. Others scheduled Byers to work against new, promising talent like Carol Cook, Kay Noble, and Lorraine Johnson.

Promoters often used June's name to draw a crowd, promising that ladies like China Mira, Cora Combs, Penny Banner, and Nell Stewart were the top contenders for June's prize. Promoters frequently sold fans on number one contender's matches, even if a championship with June Byers was not in the cards. Despite their broken relationship, Billy Wolfe was among those, hyping new teens and young adults as the future Women's Champion.

When she wasn't wrestling, June could be seen at ringside anywhere Sam was working. The former baseball hopeful was making a transition of his own from wrestler to ring announcer. June was happy to go on the road and show her support, even if that simply meant waving to the crowd from a ringside seat. Sam would return the favor when June worked, announcing his bride as she made her ring entrance.

June wrestled two opponents in one night on March 26, 1958 in Wilmington, Delaware. Incensed that Carol Cook and the venerable Mae Young had interfered with her title match against challenger Jill Hill a few weeks prior, June issued a special challenge. She bet $500 that she could pin both Cook and Young on the same night, each within thirty minutes.

The main event that night in Fournier Hall was dubbed the Iron Woman Match. The crowd was small, only 645 in attendance, but the ladies put on two impressive matches. Byers dispatched Carol Cook easily, but the contest with Mae Young went the full half hour.

Two weeks later, the three ladies returned to Wilmington along with Gloria Barratini, who had watched the Iron Woman Match from ringside. This time, all four women would compete in a tag match with Barratini working as June's partner. The champ and the opera singer easily dispatched Young and Cook.

A new claimant to the Women's World Championship appeared in April. The champion's name was Betty Garcia, and according to Knoxville booker John Cazana, Betty defeated June Byers for the title in Montreal just three weeks earlier — a remarkable accomplishment considering, as previously mentioned, women's wrestling was forbidden in Montreal.

"It was a one fall, one hour match. But for some reason the Canadian Athletic Commission so far has refused to recognize Garcia as the new queen. If they do, the National Wrestling Alliance will follow suit." Garcia was said to be threatening legal action if she was not recognized as the winner of a championship she never actually won.

June was busy defending her title on the East Coast, making televised appearances in Boston and standing up for her right to kick a little butt in the town of Pittsfield. A promoter from Troy, New York named Ted Bayly booked June and Alma Mills for the main event on a show in that Massachusetts town, but just a few days before the big event, Mayor Raymond Haughey decreed he would not allow the show to go on if women were on the card. Massachusetts had no laws against women's wrestling, but Mayor Haughey decided it would not be happening in his town.

June and Sam were living with Ted Bayley at the time while Sam worked for Bayley's weekly television production. Even though her match was canceled, she made the trek to Pittsfield so that Bayley could save face, proving to the fans that he had, in fact, booked the Women's World Champion.

Sitting in the office prior to the show, June spoke with a reporter from *The Berkshire Eagle* named Roger O'Gara. "It hurt my feelings a little. It was the first time anything like this ever happened to me."

June played the diplomat, empathizing with a mayor who, she

imagined, expected some rough, cigar-chomping women instead of Lady Wrestlers. "Oh sure, I know that many frown on lady wrestling, but you'll usually find that those who criticize it have never seen it. They regard us as freaks." June reminded O'Gara that no one had stopped her from wrestling in Boston just the week before.

The couple settled down for a bit in the Boston area as Sam worked the local, live television program. June took some time off the road during the summer and only took a handful of dates in the fall, most of them in New England.

The Inquiring Photographer Jimmy Jemail featured June in an October 17, 1958 column for the New York *Daily News*. Jemail's column featured candid answers to his question of the day, which ranged from "How do you know that you are sane?" to "Do you remember your first kiss, and did you enjoy it?" His queries often earned some strange responses and an occasional slap from a misunderstanding subject.

Suggested by a reader, Jemail asked June Byers the question, "Are you the boss or is your husband or sweetheart the boss?" June was ready with an answer.

"Let me see. My husband does all the shopping, the cooking, the house cleaning, and he walks the dogs. But come to think of it, I must be the boss after all, because even though I'm the champion, I'm just clay in his hands."

In early 1959 the Menackers relocated to Louisville, Kentucky. The Derby city provided a centralized location for the couple to work all over the Midwest, even though the local situation was in limbo. After the death of long time promoter Francis McDonogh in 1957, the Allen Athletic Club lost its regular building and was sold to a local baseball player, who had no luck reviving the weekly wrestling tradition in the newly opened fairgrounds arena, Freedom Hall.

Former wrestler turned movie star Wee Willie Davis moved to Louisville and opened his own promotion office, the Goldenrod Athletic Club. Davis became the local point man for the Indianapolis office run by Jim Barnett, but in 1959, times were tough. The Indianapolis office, under Barnett and later Dick the Bruiser, would struggle to draw an audience in Louisville. Bruiser would ultimately give up on the town, opening the door for Jerry Jarrett to claim the city for Memphis in 1970.

Sam, a licensed pilot, purchased an airplane while they were living in Louisville. June enrolled in flight lessons and earned her license flying out of Bowman Field. The couple always flew together when they could in their own plane, a huge treat after spending so many years and miles on the road.

Moolah continued to travel much more extensively, touting herself as the Women's World Champion. In many she continued to push the lie she'd defeated June Byers in many cities. In others she admitted she'd never faced June Byers but only because Byers was afraid of her.

Nevertheless, more and more promoters were turning to Moolah when they booked a ladies match. June was no longer traveling 100,000 miles a year. Moolah was willing to go anywhere, and the promoters like Leroy McGuirk, who told his fans that June Byers had simply gone inactive, gave deference to the controversial champion who was available to one that wasn't.

The wrestling press was equally split on the issue. *Wrestling Revue* continued to rank June as the number one women's wrestler as late as 1962, but *The Ring* magazine jumped on the Moolah bandwagon in 1959. Not only did they rank Moolah at number one, they placed June at third behind Moolah and Nell Stewart. By 1963 the publication ranked June at number four behind Moolah, Penny Banner, and Karen Kellogg.

Over the next few decades, a few narratives emerged as to how Moolah "won" the championship from June Byers. One version stated that June Byers lost the title to Moolah in a 1956 tournament held in Baltimore, leading to the belief she held the title for two years or 730 days. Another version said June retired in the mid-1950s, leaving the title vacant. Moolah won a women's tournament in Baltimore in 1956 and successfully defended the belt against June Byers when she came out of retirement in 1957. Moolah repeated her tales of triumph so often, it's likely she came to believe them herself.

In truth, June took some well-deserved time off and became choosy about where she wrestled and with whom. Moolah was happy to take on the territories June skipped, and she began to craft her own legend as June's successor.

She succeeded in every way except one: she never beat June Byers for the title.

THE GREAT WHITE NORTH

Most wrestlers will tell you it's more fun to be the bad guy, and no one enjoyed that role more than June Byers. But June certainly wasn't missing the heel life on a hot summer night in Newport News. Lorraine Johnson was cast in the villain's role and drew the ire of the referee — and local officials — by taking the action outside the ring on several occasions.

June returned the favor, of course, matching Johnson blow for blow in the ring and out. And as was often the case, the man selected to keep order found himself on the bottom of a three person pile as the ladies kept crashing on top of him.

The loss for Lorraine Johnson was nothing compared to what happened next. A crowd of young men followed her, hurling real trash along with the usual trash talk. Reaching the safety of the make shift dressing room set up in a fire station, Lorraine looked into the mirror and extracted the paperclip hurled by a fan into the ring that embedded itself in her shoulder.

Still, this was the life Johnson had chosen over a life on the Minnesota farm where she grew up. The youngest of five girls, Lorraine Johnson saw sports as a way out of the rural life. She had an opportunity to play professional women's basketball, but the money was better in pro wrestling.

Johnson debuted in 1950 and saw success as a single as well as a tag team, becoming Women's Tag Champion with her look-alike partner Penny Banner. Her daughter Nickla Roberts found success in the wrestling business as well, taking on the ring name Babydoll and feuding with — among others — the legendary manager Jim Cornette.

June and Lorraine dished out even more ref abuse in Nashua, New Hampshire during a tag match. Despite a very light turnout, June teamed with Laura Martinez and Lorraine with Jessica Rogers to raise some hell in a match that saw all four ladies go through the ropes. The girls, at least, were able to leave the ring fully clothed, while the ref was relieved of both shirt and pants during the fracas.

Lorraine Johnson tagged with June as well. The pair worked a few matches together in late 1959, wrestling Jackie Hammond and Judy Glover in Cincinnati and Indianapolis.

Most of June's bookings in 1959 and 1960 came from the Midwest. From August on, she went no further west than Nebraska and no further east than Cincinnati. She traveled to Wisconsin and Minnesota but worked mostly in Indiana, making her debut in the college town of Terre Haute. She never went further south than Louisville.

The Great White North continued to draw June Byers, specifically the Calgary territory of Stu Hart. The Women's World champion was one of the featured stars at the Calgary Stampede in July of 1960. Her photo appeared in the program alongside Whipper Billy Watson, Gene Kiniski, and Pat O'Connor.

June continued to take on new, younger challengers. One of the most interesting encounters was with a girl named Tona Tomah. One of the last girls trained and promoted personally by Billy Wolfe, Tomah grew up on the Whiteearth Reservation in Minnesota. Wolfe gave Tomah the title of Princess, an all too common moniker for lady wrestlers of Indigenous descent, and made sure that her skills as a ceremonial dancer were mentioned in the press.

A new generation of men was coming into its own at the time, some of whom would have a significant impact on the Midwest. June shared the spotlight on some nights with Vern Gagne, Dick the Bruiser, The Crusher, Nick Bockwinkel, The Sheik, and Angelo Poffo, father of Leaping Lanny Poffo and Randy Savage.

As their star rose, it became harder and harder for June to hang on to the spotlight. The hair-pulling, the brawls outside the ring, and the customary stripping of the referee's shirt continued, but even June Byers started to slide down the card from the main event.

The stories of June and other lady wrestlers shrank in the papers as well. Having once commanded the front page of the sports pages with large print photos and colorful narratives, you were lucky to get more than just the end result from the women's matches.

Indianapolis became Sam and June's new home, as Sam continued his transition to an on-air personality. Just a hundred miles north of their former home in Louisville, Indianapolis was an even better situation for the veteran champion who had traded her national spotlight for a smaller loop around the Midwest.

June made a four-week stand in Louisville to kick off 1961. In addition to Lorraine Johnson, Theresa Theis, and Penny Banner, she wrestled African American star Kathleen Wimbley. Louisville was on the northern edge of the Southern territories that had long prohibited blacks and whites from sharing the ring together. Just a few years after Bobo Brazil broke the color barrier in that town by wrestling Lenny Montana (Luca Brasi from *The Godfather*), Byers and Wimbley did the same on the ladies' side.

While the Indianapolis office had a strong following that would only grow in the coming years, June was no longer working the big towns like she once did. She was wrestling in Terre Haute, a college town on the western edge of the Indiana; Angola, a rural community in the extreme Northeastern corner of the state; and Seymour, a town just off the Interstate halfway between Louisville and Indianapolis. June also made some public appearances, her status as a champion and legend in the business making her a popular guest at local events in the Indianapolis area.

For the most part, June was enjoying time away from the ring. Sam's steady work with the Indianapolis office allowed her to try new things, and one of the hobbies she took up was the electric organ. She was in the right place at the right time when the *The Indianapolis Star* ran a story on May 14, 1961, about adults taking up music lessons, many for the first time. June's photo appeared in the story detailing how doctors, nurses, librarians, college professors, housewives, and yes, even lady wrestlers could learn a new instrument in their forties

172

and fifties.

June's name appeared often in papers hyping women's matches to become the number one contender, but other than a television appearance in Miami in early summer, she stayed close to home. Some papers stated June was rehabbing an injury, which may not have been completely untrue. She'd been traveling and wrestling professionally for nearly two decades. All the conditioning in the world isn't going to keep the wear and tear off one's body for so long.

Sam Menacker would become famous as the lead announcer for Dick the Bruiser's WWA based in Indianapolis years later, but his and June's journeyman days were not yet over. After a few years in the Midwest, the couple relocated north of the border when Sam signed a contract to do television in Calgary for Stu Hart.

"It was always a big deal any time June Byers came to town," says Bruce Hart, who was about ten years old at the time June and Sam moved to Calgary. "I remember her son Billy coming with them when Sam went to work with my dad."

Shirley Walsh of the *Calgary Herald* caught up with June in September of 1961. The arrival of the reigning women's champ brought a lot of buzz to a wrestling-crazed town, and June was happy to share some of her passions outside the ring.

In addition to playing the organ taking flying lessons, she enjoyed cooking and was more than a little gifted with ceramics. She was also learning the piano, and June showed Ms. Walsh the piano Sam had bought for her after the move to Canada.

In other interviews, June talked about her love of reading and languages. She started studying Spanish in the 1960s, and she read a book a week on average.

June continued to raise and breed Pekingese dogs. She continued her daily workouts as well, and she became a panelist on a television program called *Dear Wrestler*.

Sam was quite a hit himself in Calgary. A publication called *Radio-Television Daily* declared him to be the best dressed Canadian TV personality. Another publication reported that Sam had 101 suits in his wardrobe.

June co-headlined the 1962 Stampede wrestling show with Gene Kiniski on a card that also featured Argentina Rocca, Gorgeous George, and midget wrestling. As June got back to work defending her title in Western Canada, another claimant to her crown began defending a women's championship in her former stomping grounds.

Penny Banner had taken June's spot on the cards in Indiana and across the Midwest, and the story was Penny had defeated June for her title. While Penny faced June many times for the title and even earned a handful of draws, she never got a win over the champion. But in 1961, you could fabricate a mysterious title match in another town and crown a champion when needed.

June reunited with Theresa Theis to close out 1961. June defended her title against Theis all over Western Canada in November and December. In early 1963 it was Dot Dotson's turn to head north and work with June for the title. Dotson and June worked the semi-main event underneath the heavyweight champion George Scott, who was feuding with Killer Kowalski, but the ladies remained a threat to steal the show every night from Regina to Edmonton.

The champ worked only a handful of matches in the States during 1962, making appearances in Minneapolis, Indianapolis, Denver, Reno, and Toledo, where she squared off against African American pioneer Babs Wingo. Her absence from the States enabled Moolah to gain even more of a foothold. Women's wrestling was no longer the draw it had been with Mildred Burke and Billy Wolfe on top, but it was still a popular special attraction.

Some promoters were satisfied presenting "number one contender" matches for June's title, but others wanted a champion in the ring. As her nickname implied, Moolah was money, and promoters willingly sold the narrative that Moolah had unseated Byers.

In Canada June remained the undisputed champion and a huge attraction. As she had for many years, she appeared at the Calgary Stampede, wrestling one of the marquee matches at the

Stampede wrestling show. Her immense popularity opened Western Canada up to women's wrestling for good.

HOME AGAIN

The year 1963 brought another change of pace for the women's world champion. Billy Boy, now going by William, was now a student at the University of Detroit and worked for Detroit promoter, John J. Doyle. Empty nesters June and Sam boarded their private plane and set out on a vacation. Starting in January 1963, they flew to every state in the Union, except Hawaii, and even made a few stops in Mexico. It was the first vacation either of them had enjoyed for years.

The Menackers relocated to El Paso that same year. Sam went to work for Dr. Raymond Gardea, promoter of International Wrestling Enterprises. The fans were thrilled to have Sam back in town, along with the Women's World Champion. The couple not only made an immediate impact on the wrestling shows, the two dog lovers became active and outspoken members of the El Paso Kennel Club.

June spent most of her time in 1963 traveling her home state. She locked up with her former tag partner Millie Stafford along with Verne Bottoms and newer wrestlers like Maria DeLeon. She participated in some intergender tag matches, teaming with Billy White Wolf against Verne Bottoms and Jack Donovan.

June faced Jessica Rogers in St. Louis on October 11. The Portland, Oregon native was no rookie but had become a wrestler in part because of June.

"It's really a...I can't even explain it when you wrestle your idol," Jessica told Slam Wrestling's Greg Oliver. "It upset me to wrestle my idol. Of course I didn't beat her. But yeah she was great. She was my champion."

A return to the states brought renewed attention from the wrestling media. *The Ring Wrestling* published a story about June in December of 1963. Maxwell W. Goss painted a portrait of a woman who didn't know the meaning of the words, "slow down." He describes the piles of fan letters she receives; her charitable work visiting children's hospitals and speaking to boys and girls groups; her busy travel schedule; her many hobbies; and her relentless commitment to staying in top physical condition.

"One thing is for certain," Goss concludes, "There is no waste of time in June Byers' world. It is a world where determination and accomplishments are the keynotes. It is a world in which a dynamic girl wrestler who has box office magic as well as high skill travels each week to all parts of the nation. It is a world wherein she finds time to take care of her dogs, fly a plane, play an electric organ, train rigidly, and speak to groups of children. But most of all, it is a work in which June Byers, woman wrestler, creates the time to be June Byers, devoted wife and mother."

Little did anyone know that by the time the December issue of *The Ring* hit newsstands, June would be winding up her illustrious career, thanks to one bad night on the road. Near the end of 1963 June became a casualty of a passionate fan when she was hit in the head with a Coke bottle thrown from the seats. June was able to finish the match, but she was suffering double vision. Despite this impairment, she got behind the wheel of her car to head for home.

She should have known better. Auto accidents had ended the career of Elvira Snodgrass and taken the life of her friend, Mars Bennett. On the way home, June crashed her car into a tree.

June survived, but the impact crushed her knee cap and nearly crushed her right leg. June wanted to get back to the ring, but her doctors advised against it. Another break to a leg that had already taken many bumps in the ring and she would need an amputation. She had a tough choice, but after almost two decades in the ring, she made the smart decision. The time had come to hang up her boots.

June spoke about her retirement two decades later with Jim Melby, selling herself as a fighting champion until the end. "I retired on January 1st, 1964, my son's birthday. I loved the sport so much. I wanted my supporters to remember me at my peak, when I still wrestled well, and looked sharp physically. I gave the NWA six months notice of my intentions and I met all worthy contenders before I quit. I think I did both the sport and myself credit, as I didn't want to wrestle as an old woman. It wasn't a case where I was afraid of the competition, I simply wanted to keep the respect of my peers, and not be a discredit to the sport I so dearly love."

June's departure from the business, along with Billy Wolfe's death in 1963, accelerated Moolah's rise to the top. More and more promoters were willing to sign off on her as the rightful champion, furthering the false narrative she'd won the title from June Byers. Moolah told the story so many times, it became gospel.

"At the world championship tournament in Baltimore I won the title when I beat June Byers two out of three falls," said Moolah, who described the completely fabricated moments leading up to the fictional match to the New York *Daily News* in June of 1975. "I thought if I have to use my fists and feet and bite and scratch I would even if it isn't allowed. If you want something that hard you'll try anything."

Moolah wanted to be champion. She became champion. In fact she took over the business once dominated by Billy Wolfe. She became the de facto booker for nearly all of the lady wrestlers from the sixties into the nineties. Some say she even surpassed Billy Wolfe in the ways she took advantage of her girls, taking a huge chunk of their pay while also charging for room, board, and training.

The one thing Moolah never got was a match with June. She could sell the lie in the age before the Internet, but even Moolah knew the truth.

June Byers retired as champion. From August 20, 1954 until January 1, 1964, June never lost a singles match. She was pinned a few times. She lost some tag matches. She even let Penny Banner take her to a draw on occasion. But she never faced Moolah, and she never lost her title.

A classic pose of the long-reigning champion.

Battling Penny Banner in Cincinnati in 1959. Referees had to tread lightly if they didn't want to lose their shirt — or pants. Courtesy Steve Ogilvie.

Penny Banner gets the upper hand in Cincinnati 1959. Courtesy Steve Ogilvie.

June's chop was every bit as fearsome as Wahoo McDaniel's. Cincinnati 1959 with Penny Banner. Courtesy Steve Ogilvie.

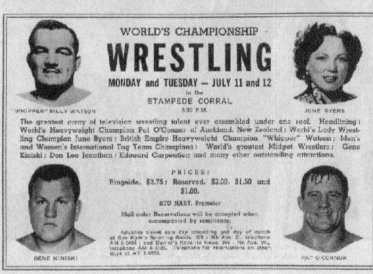

From the 1960 Calgary Stampede program. June was a regular in Calgary for many years.

Despite rumors to the contrary, June carried her belt until she retired January 1, 1964.

June left wrestling January 1, 1964 and went right into real estate. She sold homes in El Paso for several years before moving home to Houston to be closer to her family.

Top: June (bottom left) with granddaughter Kay, granddaughter Jeanne, and daughter Jewel. Bottom: June and granddaughter Kay in 1994. Photos courtesy Kay Parker.

Kay Parker and Debra Nowaski represented their grandmother at the International Pro Wrestling Hall of Fame Induction Ceremony in August of 2023.

GRANDMOTHER

When June retired from wrestling, she left the business entirely. After years of stating her desire to become a promoter, she walked away without ever giving it a shot. She still traveled a bit with Sam, making an appearance when he went to Australia in the fall of 1964, but while Sam continued to advance his career, June's interests lay elsewhere. The couple divorced, and Sam went on his way, working as a television wrestling announcer in Australia, Hawaii, Louisiana, and Hong Kong before returning to Indianapolis and Dick the Bruiser.

June wasted very little time moving on to the next phase of her life. Her name was all over the *El Paso Times* and the *El Paso Herald-Post* starting in January 1965. This time, however, readers did not see her name on the sports pages but in the classifieds. June Byers, once again a blonde, was now in the real estate business.

"Wow! World's Champion, Lady Wrestler Trying for World's Champion of Real Estate Sales and Service!" proclaimed an ad from the El Paso Times on January 28, 1965. "June has a new crown to go for 'the sale of your home.' This to her is a real challenge, and she intends to have the match (Buyer & Seller) well in hands with your help."

The staff at Town & Country, the real estate firm that employed June, had to be thrilled. Here was a sports star known all over the country. She had wrestled from coast to coast and internationally in Australia, Canada, and Mexico. She'd made television appearances on wrestling programs as well as popular quiz shows.

And now, she was El Paso's hottest new realtor.

June married an El Paso man named George Snyder, a retired Air Force veteran and the owner of G & J Automotive. Snyder had ten children of his own, six girls and four boys, who all lived in Colorado. The marriage would only last a few years, but this time, it did not end in divorce. Snyder passed away on May 5, 1970.

June Byers did not stay in El Paso after George's death. She had family in Houston, including two children who were starting to have families of their own. After nearly twenty years on the road, June wanted to spend more time with the son the public knew and the daughter she never forgot.

Wrestling can be brutal on the relationship between a parent and their children. The business is full of tragic stories of children who never knew their famous Mom or Dad, children who often rejected their parents' efforts to reconnect once their time in the spotlight was over.

Even though June never spoke publicly about her daughter Jewel, she never lost touch with her oldest child. While Ottaway and Belle Roberts raised and loved Jewel as their own, Jewel and June remained close. In her new life as a realtor, June was blessed to not only have time with her kids but a quiver full of grandkids.

Jewel and her brother William both married. William had one son, also named William. Jewel had ten children in all, the oldest and youngest being seventeen years apart in age! They all knew June as Grandmother, a title she insisted upon. As old fashioned and traditional as she could be, she refused to be addressed as Grandma, Memaw, Nana, or any such nickname.

"I was the only exception in our house," says Kay Parker, the youngest of Jewel's children. "Everyone else had to call her Grandmother, but I knew her as June Bug. Years later, when I connected with my cousin Wil, I found out he called her June Bug as well."

June was exceptionally proud of her son. He had finished college, married, and had a son of his own. But on October 13, 1972, she received a call with the most horrific news a mother could ever hear. William Byers, her beloved "Billy Boy," was gone.

William was installing a dishwasher and a vent hood over a stove when he was electrocuted. He was only 30 years of age. June would outlive her son by another 26 years, but she would never be the same.

In spite of her grief, June found joy in watching her many grandchildren grow up. Those who knew the never-conquered Women's World Wrestling Champion as Grandmother have many fond memories of her.

June often railed against the crude, rough image of women wrestlers to the press while portraying herself as a true, genteel lady. Her grandchildren confirm the lady image was no act! June was a true Southern lady right to her core. She was intelligent, well-versed, and always well-dressed. She abhorred swearing, deeming cuss words to be a sign of being uneducated, and never used such language herself.

"June's home was always pristine, and her yard," says Jewel's oldest child Debra Nowaski. "She loved feeding her birds and sitting on her back patio and visiting. She also loved iced tea."

"She had a regular group of friends who came over to play cards," adds Kay Parker. "She was very good at cards."

June loved to regale her grandkids with stories from the road. She talked about her workout routine, about running alongside her car while traveling, and drinking so much orange juice she smelled like orange blossoms. The orange juice habit stayed with her the rest of her life, and the scent of orange blossoms still reminds her grandchildren of her.

Her granddaughters were obviously quite fascinated by Grandmother's past history and often asked the question, "Is it real?"

Grandmother was ready with an answer. "The pain was real. The moves are real. The training is real."

To this she added, "Anything I can do in the ring, I can do out of the ring." With a mischievous smile, she'd then ask her granddaughters, "DO YOU WANT TO WRESTLE?"

June found love one last time. On November 25, 1980, she married a Houston man named Oscar W. Stone. Less than four years, later, the couple split, with the divorce becoming final on June 22, 1984.

That same year, June gave an extensive interview to wrestling journalist Jim Melby, an interview that's been referenced many times in this book. Melby asked Byers if she missed the roar of the crowd. "I don't know, but I did at one time. In fact I thought about making a comeback, but I was involved in an automobile accident where I was seriously injured. That changed my plans as I was in the hospital for months, and on crutches for eighteen months. I did enjoy the adulation of the crowd, but I knew that I had to put that part of my life behind me."

Melby asked, "If you had to go back in time and do it all over again, would you?"

June was emphatic. "Yes, I loved every minute of it."

Byers was working as director of the first Yurika family center in the U.S. "Yurika foods aren't health foods per se, but they certainly are healthy foods for you. I also have a real estate license. I apply myself to business the same as I did to wrestling, I strive to be the best. For the first time in my life I had a home that is mine, my roots."

"Do people recognize you as a former wrestler?" Melby asked.

"Yes, people do. Recently a lady came up to me and asked if it was true if I used to be a lady wrestler. When I told her it was true she said that I looked too pretty to be a wrestler. That type of statement has always stayed with me. Some of the most beautiful women athletes that I've seen over the years have been lady wrestlers. I might add that many of the male wrestlers are also attractive."

Melby also asked June what advice she'd give to a woman who aspired to become a pro wrestler. "First I would ask them if becoming a wrestler was what they wanted more in life than anything else. If they said yes, I'd encourage them, but warn them about all of the sacrifices, both physical and mental, that they would have to make. I believe that they would have to train very hard, as conditioning is 90% of an athlete's success. The other important ingredient is desire and dedication. Any girl planning a career in the ring had best set her goals to reach for the top, to always wrestle to win."

JUNE REMEMBERED

June Byers made the *Houston Chronicle* in 1988. It was a sweet story not about her, but about her 71-year-old sister Susie, who had found love after praying and placing an ad in the personals of the newspaper. Bill Sharp, 82, just happened to glance at the personals that day and read about the blue-eyed, active woman seeking someone who liked traveling, dancing, and going to church. The couple had their first date at International House of Pancakes. A few dates later, they were married in Susie's church.

"They look, and act, 10 to 15 years younger now than before they met," said June, who admitted she cried during the wedding. "I haven't seen Susie happier in years."

June enjoyed her latter years surrounded by grandchildren and a growing number of great-grandchildren. She also stayed connected to her wrestling family and attended a few reunions with the Cauliflower Alley Club and LIWA — the Ladies International Wrestling Association founded by, of all people, The Fabulous Moolah.

"June was always a beautiful woman, even when we saw her in Los Angeles at the Cauliflower Alley Club Convention a few years back," said Theresa Theis. "She really brought herself up a whole life, and always tried to improve her mind by reading everything and playing Scrabble while on the road. She always had respect for the other wrestlers and we all had respect for her too, of course."

Fans who never got to see June wrestle enjoyed meeting the unconquered champion as well. New England promoter Sheldon Goldberg had his opportunity to shake June's hand at a LIWA convention. "When I first learned about June Byers, I was struck by how much her photos looked like my mother when she was young," says Goldberg. "She was, of course, older when I met her, but she had aged in all the same ways my mother had. She was still selling real estate at the time, and she was a very sweet lady."

Around 1994 June's family noticed she was struggling with her memory. Kay Parker, June's youngest grandchild, was a newlywed, and the couple went to a family gathering at June's house. "She went around the room and came to my husband and said, 'Thank you for coming. Who are you and who are you here with? That was the beginning."

June was diagnosed with dementia. As her condition deteriorated, an old colleague from Western Canada arrived to lend support — though the quality of that support was questionable. Bob Sweetan first crossed paths with June in the early 1960s when the Saskatchewan native was just getting started under Stu Hart. Sweeten saw her success with Stampede, the NWA, and the World Wrestling Council in Puerto Rico. He worked heel and is said to have been a major influence on Shawn Michaels.

Sweetan was not well-loved in the wrestling community. Both Jim Ross and Jim Duggan described the man as a bully, with Ross adding he was generally a miserable human being. In 1990 Sweetan was convicted of sexually assaulting his own daughter, and he was in constant trouble with Canadian authorities for not paying child support.

"He was an ass," says Kay Parker, who saw Sweetan as a man taking advantage of her grandmother's condition. "He said he was there to help her, but I think he was a loser and didn't have anywhere else to live. He was just using her money."

June may have been ill, but she wised up in time to kick Bob Sweeten to the curb before she passed. Sweetan was deported back to Canada in 2000 after he stopped checking in regularly with the police. He died in a British Columbia nursing home in 2017.

Another wrestler moved in after Sweetan. June's family no longer remembers his name, but they remember him being a much kinder, gentler soul than Sweetan. He stayed with June until the end.

The great June Byers fell ill with pneumonia in the summer of 1998. June passed away quietly on July 20, 1998, Kay Parker's father's birthday.

June was laid to rest in South Park Cemetery, located in Pearland, Texas. The simple marker bore the name Dealva E. Snyder, a nod to the one husband she did not divorce, George Snyder. Beneath her legal name, the family had the name wrestling fans everywhere knew: JUNE BYERS.

June was gone before the cameras began to roll on the 2004 film *Lipstick and Dynamite*, a documentary about the legendary women of wrestling. Despite her lengthy reign as champion, June received very little mention. Most of it focused on how stiff she was in the ring.

Many of the participants, including Penny Banner, found it frustrating how much of their stories, including positive recollections of Billy Wolfe, were left out of the final cut. The Fabulous Moolah used the film as a platform to further her own legend as the greatest women's champion, but she stopped short of lying one last time about how she had become a champion. When asked by the director of the documentary *Lipstick and Dynamite* who she beat to become champion, Moolah didn't give a name. She just said she beat the women's champion.

While working on his biography of Mildred Burke, Pulitzer Prize-winning author Jeff Leen came to see June as a bit "mean and mercenary." He cited how quickly she moved from Billy Wolfe to G. Bill to Sam Menacker, each a man who could further her career, as evidence of her mercenary nature. Nevertheless, Leen acknowledged June was in a class by herself.

"I do believe that June was probably the most physically gifted of the female wrestlers of her generation, blessed with size, speed, strength, great flexibility and superb technical ability. A rare and powerful combination of abilities. The Byers Bridge is evidence of all of that. She was such a freak of nature that she could have beaten or at least been credible against the male pros of that era in a shoot match if they didn't have too much of a size advantage."

In 2006 the Professional Wrestling Hall of Fame, then located in New York State, became the first wrestling hall of fame to induct June. She was the fifth woman honored by that institution following Mildred Burke, The Fabulous Moolah, Mae Young, and Penny Banner. The Hall of Fame relocated to Wichita Falls, Texas and has since closed under somewhat mysterious circumstances.

In 2017 June and Judy Grable were part of the second class of "Legacy" inductions to the WWE Hall of Fame. Prior to 2016, the virtual hall of fame created by the World Wrestling Entertainment only honored men and women who had played a significant role in the WWE and its previous incarnations, the World Wrestling Federation (WWF) and Worldwide Wrestling Federation (WWWF). Legacy inductions have since broadened the scope of the hall of fame, acknowledging the careers of men and women who made a major impact on pro wrestling outside the WWE. Cora Combs was inducted in 2018, and Ethel Johnson followed in 2021.

Sadly, the WWE does not even notify the families of its legacy inductees, much less invite them to the induction ceremony. June's family found out about the honor through the Internet, the same way Barbara Goodish and Karen McDaniel found out their deceased husbands Bruiser Brody and Wahoo McDaniel were being honored. Ethel Johnson's family suffered and added insult. Not only were they not told of Johnson's induction, the WWE accidentally used a photo of Sandy Parker during the video montage honoring Johnson.

The new International Pro Wrestling Hall of Fame located in New York state was happy to invite June's family to participate in honoring their matriarch in August of 2023. Granddaughters Debra Nowaski and Kay Parker flew from Houston to Albany to accept the honor for their beloved grandmother. June joined a class of standout talents that included Gorgeous George, Bret Hart, Verne Gagne, Dr. B.F. Roller, and Keiji Muto. While June was preceded by Mildred Burke in joining the IPWHOF, she is the second woman to be inducted into the brand new hall of fame.

The IPWHOF also honored another woman June would have

admired greatly in 2023. While her son Jerry Jarrett was the boss of the Memphis territory during the latter part of her career in wrestling, Christine "Teeny" Jarrett was the boss on the road. Teeny managed the shows in Louisville, Evansville, and wherever the road took her each week. She commanded respect from everyone from Jerry Lawler to Dutch Mantell. The IPWHOF bestowed the Trailblazer Award on Ms. Jarrett, a woman who succeeded in a man's world and truly made her mark on the business.

In 2023 filmmaker Ash Avildsen partnered with legendary wrestling broadcaster Jim Ross to bring Mildred Burke's biography *Queen of the Ring* to the screen. Filmed in Louisville, Kentucky, the movie brought such legendary lady wrestlers to life as Mildred Burke, Mae Young, Nell Stewart, Babs Wingo, Ethel Johnson, Marva Scott, Gladys Gillem, Elvira Snodgrass, and of course, June Byers. Byers was portrayed by a woman who was one of her true successors, NWA Women's Champion Kamille Brickhouse.

The climactic battle between June Byers and Mildred Burke (played by Emily Bett Rickards) was filmed at Actor's Theater of Louisville over three nights in July of 2023. Seated at ringside on those hot summer nights were Ohio Valley Wrestling's long time announcer Dean Hill, Jim Cornette as the NWA Commissioner, and Martin Kove as promoter Al Haft. Right behind the trio sat an extra who had traveled almost a thousand miles to see Kamille bring her grandmother to life, June's granddaughter Kay Parker.

Scott Romer, an Indianapolis native and world-renowned photographer, became close friends with June's fourth husband Sam Menacker. Romer met Menacker in the 1970s when he was just a teenager taking photos at Dick the Bruiser's shows with his buddy David McLane, who later created the women's wrestling promotions GLOW and WOW.

Romer never found acceptance from his father and quickly adopt Sam Menacker as one of his surrogate fathers. Sam gave Scott a ride to the show every week, and Romer would soak up all the knowledge Sam was willing to share. Sam even came to Romer and

McLane's school when they staged a wrestling show for elementary students, complete with fake blood. Menacker was the ring announcer for the event, and despite a lecture he delivered after seeing the fake blood, the boys knew he was delighted with what he saw.

As close as they became, Sam Menacker never spoke to Scott Romer about June Byers. If he harbored any ill will or hurt feelings over their failed marriage, he kept it to himself. But in June of 1983, Menacker's affection for Byers was evident in a column he wrote for *The Wrestling News* addressing the question of whether or not June ever lost her title.

"I have heard many older (and retired) wrestlers say how many tough guys they had defeated, even if they had never wrestled them. I suppose that people always like to put their best foot forward. Possibly there is no harm done, when, for example, a father tells his young son, how great he (the father) was when he played football or wrestled. But there are times when a wrestler might claim victories over a star of the past, which would besmirch the reputation of that particular top name."

Sam recounted hearing many a man claim to have once defeated the great men's champion Lou Thesz, claims that had no basis in reality and could never be substantiated. Then he turned his attention to June Byers.

"Sometimes we read stories of how she had been defeated. I'm sure that when she first started wrestling there may have been a time when she was not always a winner. But she had that great determination which brought her to the very top in her chosen profession. No one could ever match her accomplishments. She developed a wrestling maneuver known as the 'Byers Bridge.' With this intricate hold she won many hundreds of bouts. The hold is difficult to apply, but when June used it, it meant victory. No wrestler, man or woman, has been able to use that hold."

June had a hard road to the top. She tasted defeat many times as she worked her way up from preliminary matches to the main event. She logged thousands of miles on the road. She suffered numerous injuries, working through most of them so she did not lose her spot.

She paid her dues.

She became the Women's World Champion.

And no one ever took that title away from her.

"From August 1954 to her retirement in 1964, June wrestled every top contender and remained victorious. No one defeated her. In memory's eye, we see her in dazzling beauty, as the ring announcer says, "…and now, ladies and gentlemen… it is my privilege to introduce the world's champion lady wrestler, THE GREAT AND INIMITABLE JUNE BYERS!!!"

ACKNOWLEDGEMENTS

First and foremost, a special thank you to Debra Nowaski and Kay Parker, June Byers' granddaughters, for their stories, photos, and blessing on this project. For many years, these lovely ladies and their relatives have had to hear only the "bad" about their beloved Grandmother. Now her full story can be told.

Thank you to grandson Wil Byers, who shared some wonderful photos of his grandmother for the book, including the Byers Bridge photo on the back cover.

Thank you to Betsy Wolfe and Mickie-Mae Johnson, daughters of G. Bill and Betsy Wolfe and granddaughters of Billy Wolfe. It's an honor to share the story of your parents' love and your amazing family.

A huge thank you to Chris Bergstrom, founder of the Facebook group known as the Fabulous Ladies of Wrestling. Chris's work has shed a great deal of light on the golden age of women's wrestling, and his contributions to this volume include information on Mattie Bell, Ann LaVerne, Violet Viann, and many, many, many more. Chris also colorized the photos for the cover.

A big debt of thanks goes to Jeff Leen, author of the Mildred Burke biography *Queen of the Ring*. His book was an invaluable source of information on June's story where it intersected with Millie's, and his additional insights on June quoted in these pages are much appreciated.

Likewise, the late Penny Banner's autobiography *Banner Days* had plenty of anecdotes about June and their rivalry.

Thank you to Greg Oliver for opening up his archives and sharing his research and interview quotes about June, and also for putting me in touch with Jeff Leen.

Thanks to Pat Laprade for his insights on wrestling in and around Montreal.

Thanks to Jason Presley for fact-checking and uncovering the story behind the unfortunate demise of Henry Byers.

Thank you to my proofreaders Michael Ewing and Ian Jedlica.

Thank you to Kailey Latimer, who not only wrote the foreword for the book but brought June to life in the Mildred Burke biopic. Yes, she's the heavy in the movie, but now you know the other side of that story.

A huge thank you to my fellow June Byers enthusiast Tamaya Greenlee for all her help, encouragement, and support on this project. I wish you all the best in your world travels, though I'll probably hate you for a day or two when you're seeing Wrestle Kingdom LIVE in Japan.

Additional thanks and appreciation goes to Tom Burke, Steve Ogilvie, Mad Man Pondo, Sheldon Goldberg, Ash Avildsen, Bob Johnson, Bruce Hart, Vance Nevada, Velvet McIntyre, "Princess" Vicki Otis, Brad LaFave, Derek Spruill, Billie Starkz, Marcella Robinette, Sydney Moore, Desiree Williams, Carrie Canatsey, and Carmine DeSpirito.

Thanks to my wife Jessica, my kids Sam and Lydia, for always loving and supporting me.

Shout out to Mickey's, the wonderful coffee shop/ bookstore on Vincennes Street in New Albany, Indiana where I wrote a huge chunk of this book during the month of — you guessed it — June 2023.

Printed in Great Britain
by Amazon